A Primer of Behavior Modification

W. W. Wenrich
Roanoke College

Brooks/Cole Publishing Company
Belmont, California
A Division of Wadsworth Publishing Company, Inc.

To Four Dear Little People

Budge
Manny
Minnesota Fats
Mean Minney

L.C. Cat. Card No.: 73-113800
Printed in the United States of America

1 2 3 4 5 6 7 8 9 10 − 74 73 72 71 70

Acknowledgements

I would like to thank the many students and psychologist-colleagues who read the original manuscript and provided the almost innumerable criticisms and constructive comments that helped to improve the book. For their helpful reviews, I would particularly like to thank Dr. D. D. Cahoon of Auburn University, Robert Marrone of Sacramento State College, and R. W. McIntire of the University of Maryland.

Additionally, I would be engaged in the most self-defeating sort of maladaptive behavior if I did not give a strong acknowledgement to the wide variety of intellectual and inspirational attentions freely mediated by one of my kinder critics. With this in view, I offer the following very adaptive verbal response: Thank you, Miss F. F. Shellenberger.

Appreciation is also extended to the following authors and publishers, who kindly granted permission to quote from their materials:

T. Ayllon, Intensive treatment of psychotic behavior by stimulus satiation and food reinforcement. *Behaviour Research and Therapy*, 1963, *1* 53-69. Reprinted by permission of Pergamon Press, Inc.

W. Isaacs, J. Thomas, and I. Goldiamond, Application of operant conditioning to reinstate verbal behavior in psychotics. *Journal of Speech and Hearing Disorders*, 1960, *25*, 8-12. Reprinted by permission of the American Speech and Hearing Association.

Contents

7

**The Behavior Modification
Movement 71**

A Primer of Behavior Modification

Introduction

This book is intended for anyone who has an interest in the practical prediction and control of human behavior. While the studies reported in each chapter are addressed specifically to the modification of maladaptive behavior, the principles of conditioning on which effective modification is based are universal. These principles apply to all behavior, adaptive as well as maladaptive, and to all people. The particular attention given to the alteration of the behavior of disturbed individuals involved a choice based on the pervasiveness of the "mental health" problem in this society—a problem for which new solutions are being offered through the behavior modification movement. For the first time in history the laws of respondent and operant conditioning, which have been derived from a sound scientific discipline, are being systematically applied in the effective and dramatic amelioration of many forms of human distress.

The book is self-contained, as it requires no knowledge of psychology other than that obtained through an introductory course. Every principle employed by a given behavior modification technique is developed in detail and gradually expanded in the initial part of each chapter. The efficacy of each fundamental principle is then demonstrated through a review of research and case histories taken from the relevant psychological literature.

A few observations pertaining to the style, tenor, and order of the primer should provide the reader with a perspective that will facilitate his progress through the following pages. First of all, the book is quite didactic and assumes a strong pro-behavior modification position. As a result, and as intended, many sweeping statements are made that are subject to debate by reasonable men holding rather opposite views. It is thought that the fairly aggressive style used throughout the text is justified on the grounds that the book is designed to outline a specific orientation. The subject is behavior modification from the viewpoint of one of its staunch proponents. Stress and emphasis are also given to the importance of empiricism and of the empirical process as the final arbiter. Further, the Selected Readings section at the end of each chapter does provide the serious student with a means to expand his knowledge of particular issues and views.

Second, it should be noted that the most basic variables and principles of conditioning are presented in a simple, elementary manner—a manner which increases the probability that the reader will gain a clear understanding of these principles and a full appreciation of their importance and general application. It has been the author's experience that the usual rendering of conditioning and learning (in standard texts on this subject) often leaves the student with an uneasiness that is borne out when the examination day has arrived and his responses have been graded. The approach taken in this book places great weight on simplicity of expression without diminishing the integrity of the subject.

It should also be noted that there is great variation in the development, explanation, and definition of terms in the text. Those terms most pertinent to the basic variables and principles of conditioning are developed with great care and in considerable detail. In most cases a precise, technical definition is also offered. The care awarded these terms is tendered because they are central to the book, and because they provide the substratum for nearly all of the techniques that the behavior technologist has at hand. Other terms are handled with much less precision, either because they are assumed to constitute a portion of the reader's repertoire or because their explication in the text itself would not foster or advance the general aim of the primer. There are also many terms in the text which are common to the jargon of the psychologist but which may have slipped from the student's repertoire since he completed introductory psychology. Rather than define *ego, phobia, schizophrenia*, and similar concepts in the body of the text, the author has explained and defined such terms in the Glossary.

The order of the book is based on a progression from the more basic principles of conditioning, and from the simpler models of behavior modification, to the more complex. For this reason, the author decided to review the respondent therapies early in the text and then to consider modification procedures based on operant conditioning techniques. One note of caution should be made regarding this ordering. Implosive therapy, since it is representative of one of the most rudimentary models of behavior change—namely, respondent extinction—is first in line for review. This primacy of position (and this is the note of caution) is entirely a function of implosive therapy's simplicity rather than of its relative status in the eyes of professional personnel. Actually this technique is very new, and it remains controversial. Further, its efficacy as an effective behavior modification technique is in question at the moment, because it is in need of more well-designed research. Even so, it is a behavior therapy technique which is gaining increasing attention, and empirical tests of its feasibility and therapeutic value will determine its place in the behavior modification movement. Therefore, even though implosive therapy is controversial, it does warrant coverage in this primer.

A final comment should be made regarding the scope and purpose of the text. It is not intended that the reader, no matter how conscientiously he pores over these pages, should emerge as a competent behavior technologist. However, any reader with an inclination to understand the basis of behavior modification should finish this primer with a thorough appreciation of the nature, orientation, and applications of this new and exciting movement.

1

Subject Domain

In recent years a great deal of interest has been expressed in the application of conditioning principles to the prediction and control of human behavior. Novels with this theme continue to sell widely; academic and professional societies with this orientation are flourishing; and texts in this domain are being published at an exceptionally high rate. The attention, in most instances, is centered on the principles of operant and respondent conditioning and on the extension of these principles to the modification of behavior. This primer is intended to demonstrate how these principles are currently being applied in a rather specific, and very important, area of human activity: the modification of maladaptive human behavior.

Respondent and Operant Behavior

The subject of this book, then, is *behavior*: the ways people *react* to their environment and what they *do* to their environment. Within this context, we will attend primarily to maladaptive behaviors, which frequently precipitate an individual's commitment to a rehabilitative program. For purposes of prediction and control, psychologists find it useful to delineate two types of behavior, *respondent* and *operant*. The first type, respondent behavior, is nearly synonymous with the layman's concept of an involuntary, elicited, or automatic response, and it is mediated by the autonomic nervous system. Respondent behavior includes, for instance, salivation when a lemon drop is placed in one's mouth, "tearing" when a sand pebble

is caught in one's eye, and "startling" when one hears a loud, unantici-
pated noise. More pertinent to our subject, however, respondent behavior
also involves all of the uncomfortable and sometimes incapacitating emotional responses such as anger, guilt, fear, and anxiety—the emotional
responses which provide the substructure for the wide variety of reactions
which have traditionally been called neurotic.

In contrast to respondent behaviors (respondents), operant behaviors
(operants) are similar to the layman's concept of voluntary, "purposeful"
responses. They are mediated by the central nervous system and include
those behaviors that interact with and have an effect on the environment
of the organism. The essential characteristic of operant behavior is represented by the word "do." "Doing" includes walking and talking, fighting
and playing. "Doing" includes "schizoid" withdrawal and the "pathological" tirade. It encompasses much of the ongoing, daily behavior of a person in commerce with other persons, as well as the individual's interaction
with his general environment. A note which is relevant at this point is that,
while appearing voluntary and at times even capricious, an operant lends
itself to the same precision of prediction and control as a respondent.
When the variables that are functionally related to a specified operant are
identified and manipulated, the behavior under consideration can be predicted and controlled.

One final distinction between respondents and operants should help the
reader maintain a delineation of these two types of behavior. This distinction relates to the variables which are involved in the *practical* control of
the respective responses. A respondent is controlled by an eliciting stimulus; and the presentation of an eliciting stimulus is all that is usually
required for the occurrence of the response. The control of an operant
response, in contrast, is often a function of more than one variable. While
operants are modified *primarily* through their environmental *consequences*, their probability of occurrence may also be dependent upon
some "drive" condition or an antecedent stimulus.

Laws and Behavior

In order to understand how the scientist's power to predict and control is
developed in behavior modification, it is necessary that one appreciate
certain differences among the variables studied. That which a scientist is
interested in predicting and controlling may be labeled the *dependent variable*; and, as given in the prior section, the behavior technologist's dependent variable is behavior. If, for example, one were to investigate the
effects of adult attention upon a 6-year-old child's over-aggressive behavior, "over-aggressiveness" could be described as the dependent variable.
Upon what does the dependent variable depend? In this example, it is seen

to "depend" upon adult attention. The events, occurrences, or things of which dependent variables are a function—such as "adult attention" in the example—are termed *independent variables*.

Laws are statements of the empirical relationships between dependent and independent variables. When the laws in a given area of knowledge are known, one can then predict, control, and explain the dependent variables in that scientific area. For example, if we are given an independent variable, we can predict the occurrence of a particular dependent variable— provided that a law governing such a relationship is known. If we can manipulate an independent variable, then we are able to control the dependent variable. Also, if we are given a dependent variable, we can explain its occurrence by reference to relevant independent variables and to the lawful relationship that obtains between the two kinds of variables. This, then, represents the foundation of a scientific approach to the study of behavior. The basic variables of the subject matter are to be identified and described, and the covariations between the independent and dependent variables are to be discovered and cataloged.

Some of the major independent variables germane to the practical prediction and modification of maladaptive behavior include reinforcement, stimulus control, deprivation-satiation, and the aversive stimulus. When such variables, operationally defined, are systematically manipulated, it is possible to deal with behavior with the sort of precision which at one time was thought to be limited to the physical sciences. While the exact parameters of these variables remain to be established, current behavior technology is now able to explain and modify maladaptive responses in a way not possible even a few years ago.

Those psychologists who embrace the behavior modification model in the alteration of maladaptive behavior have followed the ground rules of *radical behaviorism* in building a scientifically respectable system involving the behavior of organisms. This approach has led to several restrictions and assumptions—specifically in regard to the locus of the major independent variables—which may be new to one who is unacquainted with this approach. For example, terms such as *will, mind, soul,* and *idea*—and other terms in a similar vein, such as *id, ego,* and *superego*—are rejected as variables in a behavioristic system. However interesting such concepts might be in some contexts, they do not typically lend themselves to rigorous scientific examination or analysis. Though it is true historically and contemporarily that man has alluded to internal events in his account of behavior, these allusions have at best been very inefficient, and they have seldom offered any success in practical prediction and control. Explanations based upon internal events or entities have little value in prediction and control, not primarily because of vagueness or of their fictional, ad hoc character,

[handwritten margin note:] discarded only on this basis; not because they don't exist or because they are totally worthless concepts.

but rather because the most important variables of which behavior is a function are to be found elsewhere. Their locus is in the organism's external world. One of the better explications of this orientation was given by B. F. Skinner (1953), the most prominent advocate of this position:

> The external variables of which behavior is a function provide for what may be called a causal or functional analysis. We undertake to predict and control the behavior of the individual organism. This is our 'dependent variable'—the effect for which we are to find the cause. Our 'independent variables'—the causes of behavior—are the external conditions of which behavior is a function. Relations between the two—the 'cause and effect relationships' in behavior—are the laws of science. A synthesis of these laws expressed in quantitative terms yields a comprehensive picture of the organism as a behaving system (p. 35).

The Format

Throughout the remaining pages of this book, we will discuss current, representative research and case studies in the modification of maladaptive human behavior. The basic variables of which behavior is a function, along with the attendant operations and principles related to these variables, are given in the chapter sub-headings. The research and studies discussed under a given chapter were selected to demonstrate how the variables or principles relevant to the chapter operate in the alteration of behavior. Consequently, in Chapters 2 and 3 we will look at therapies based upon respondent principles of conditioning, extinction, and counterconditioning. We will begin with a new and promising approach known as implosive therapy. Then we will turn to one of the rather well-established techniques of reciprocal inhibition: systematic desensitization.

In Chapter 4 we will begin our consideration of the modification of operant behavior by examining the nature and efficacy of positive reinforcement, shaping, reinforcement schedules, and related manipulations of positive reinforcers in operant conditioning. Chapter 5 will continue our exploration of operant behavior and will center on the role of the aversive stimulus, including escape and avoidance behavior, negative reinforcement, and the effects of punishment. The concluding chapter on operant behavior, Chapter 6, will cover the two remaining basic variables, stimulus control and deprivation-satiation, as well as the effectiveness of each variable in therapeutic programs. The final section of the book, Chapter 7, will be devoted to an overview of the contemporary status of behavior modification and to a prospectus on the future of this movement.

With respect to the many variations of behavior therapy or behavior modification techniques, this book is not encyclopedic—nor is it meant to be. It is intended to present *representative* techniques of all the major kinds of conditioning approaches in this domain, and it offers a *sample* of the tremendously wide range of human problems and disturbances to which conditioning has been successfully applied. More importantly, this book does elucidate all of the *major* variables of respondent and operant conditioning upon which this new behavioral movement is based, and it will suggest to the reader the limitless innovations which will emerge as the movement continues to gather momentum. Thus, the primary concerns of this primer are (1) the alignment of techniques and research with the basic variables and (2) a synthesis of the current activity in the modification of maladaptive human behavior.

Selected Readings

There are two very recent books that give rather comprehensive accounts of radical behaviorism, the systematic psychology alluded to in this chapter. The primary advantages of the first work may be found in its sophistication and its readability, as well as in the thoroughness with which it explicates the system and viewpoint on which this primer is based. For the "hurried" reader who would like a concise and adequate presentation of conditioning and related principles, the second text is recommended.

> Lundin, R. W. *Personality: A behavioral analysis.* New York: Macmillan, 1969.

> Reynolds, G. S. *A primer of operant conditioning.* Glenview, Ill.: Scott, Foresman, 1968.

If brevity is at a premium and the reader would still like a bit more background information, one or more of the following articles should prove worthwhile supplements:

> Baer, D. M., Wolf, M. M., & Risley, T. R. Some current dimensions of applied behavior analysis. *Journal of Applied Behavior Analysis,* 1968, 1, 91-97.

> Bandura, A. Psychotherapy as a learning process. *Psychological Bulletin,* 1961, 58, 143-159.

> Michael, J., & Meyerson, L. A behavioral approach to counseling and guidance. *Harvard Educational Review,* 1962, 32, 382-402.

2 Modification of Respondent Behavior: Implosion

Respondent Conditioning and Extinction

Respondent behavior, as we saw in Chapter 1, is stimulus-elicited behavior that is mediated by the autonomic nervous system. People with an appetite salivate as they take a portion of food, and they experience pain if they come into contact with an aversive surface such as a very hot dinner plate. These are examples of respondents, and in these two instances we are dealing with unconditioned responses—innate reactions to certain kinds of stimulation. Unconditioned respondents do not depend on the past history of the organism; quite to the contrary, any intact organism will have these responses as part of his behavioral repertoire. An unconditioned response (UCR), in other words, depends solely on the presentation of some specific stimulus to a biologically healthy organism. When a response is an unconditioned one, the stimulus that is sufficient to elicit that response is known as an unconditioned stimulus (UCS). In reference to our example, when a bite of food (UCS) is presented to a person, the presence of food in the person's mouth is sufficient to elicit salivation (UCR).

However, it is also the case that stimuli associated with eating food—for instance, the invitation "dinner is ready" or the sight of a well-prepared meal—will also elicit salivation. In like manner, stimuli associated with a hot plate—for example, the warnings "watch out" or "keep your hand off that hot plate"—will elicit fear, which is a conditioned response to pain. In these cases the responses are learned and do depend on a particular history, without which neither the invitation nor the warning would have any effect. Learning of this sort is called *respondent conditioning,* and it is of central importance to the behavior modification techniques discussed in this chapter and the next—techniques based on the assumption that most psychological disturbances are instances of this kind of learning.

To expedite an understanding of respondent conditioning, let us consider an extremely simple illustration—one that may function as a prototype when we examine the more complex cases involving the conditioning therapies. Suppose first that we administer a brief but painful electric shock, an unconditioned stimulus (UCS), to the finger of an experimental subject. The electric shock will elicit a number of autonomic reactions from the subject, including pain, which is an unconditioned response (UCR). Suppose now that, along with the shock, we present a tone or any other neutral stimulus to our subject. After a few pairings of tone and shock, the tone becomes a conditioned stimulus (CS) and will elicit fear, one of the concomitant autonomic responses to pain. When fear is elicited solely by the presentation of a conditioned stimulus (the tone alone), it is called a conditioned response or respondent (CR). Learning has taken place, respondent conditioning has occurred; and now the tone, a formerly neutral stimulus, will itself elicit at least part of the response (fear) which in the past was elicited by the unconditioned stimulus (shock). This procedure might be clarified through the following paradigm:

(1) UCS (shock) → elicits → UCR (pain and fear)

(2) CS (tone)
       ↓
  (paired with)
       ↓
  UCS (shock) → elicits → UCR (pain and fear)

(3) CS (tone) → elicits → CR (fear)

This paradigm shows the fundamental principle of *respondent conditioning,* which can be stated as follows: After a neutral stimulus has been paired with a stimulus which elicits a specific response, then the neutral stimulus will also elicit that response, or part of that response. Along with this principle, we should also consider a related concept—one that has a role in conditioned emotional reactions. This concept, *stimulus generalization,* refers to the fact that stimuli similar to a conditioned stimulus will also elicit the conditioned response, though to a lesser degree than the conditioned stimulus itself. For example, if the conditioned stimulus is a

1000-cycle tone, and if the conditioned response is fear, then an 800- or a 1200-cycle tone will also make the subject uneasy—but to a smaller extent than the conditioned stimulus itself, the 1000-cycle tone. As an illustration of this concept, consider this case: A woman, after having been subjected to a severely frightening experience (UCS) in an elevator which had stalled between floors, developed an intense fear (CR) of elevators (CS). Through the process of stimulus generalization, it is very likely that many other small enclosed places similar to elevators would also make her uncomfortable. The importance of this concept will become apparent a little later in this chapter.

As stated earlier, according to those who conduct research and therapy within the framework of behavior modification, the respondent conditioning paradigm is a model for the development of most learned emotions, the learned fears and phobias, the learned guilts and angers which bring individuals to an installation or clinic for treatment. In order to appreciate how and why the behavior technologist prescribes a particular program of treatment when he thinks a conditioned emotional reaction is at the root of a client's distress, we should take another look at the respondent conditioning paradigm with a view to the question of how learned respondents are eliminated. Decades of experiments and laboratory investigations have provided two basic approaches to the efficient elimination of conditioned respondents. The first of these is called extinction, and it forms the basis of implosion, the therapy to be reviewed later in this chapter. The second approach to the elimination of conditioned emotional reactions is called counterconditioning, the procedure central to reciprocal inhibition, which is discussed in Chapter 3. It is to the first of these, extinction, that we now turn our attention.

Extinction

While a conditioned stimulus may elicit a conditioned response in the absence of the unconditioned stimulus with which it was originally paired, and while it may continue to do so for a long time, eventually the conditioned response will undergo *extinction.* That is, if the CS is presented over and over again without any further pairing with the UCS, the CR will begin to diminish and finally will cease to occur at all. The tone, in the third step of our paradigm, will initially produce fear whenever it is presented; but if the tone is not occasionally paired with shock, the fear elicited by the onset of the tone will begin to decrease and eventually will not occur. Extinction is the technical term for this process, and it refers to the decrease in a conditioned respondent as the result of repeated presentation of the conditioned stimulus in the absence of the unconditioned stimulus.

An additional aspect of extinction, related to the concept of stimulus generalization, should be introduced at this juncture. Just as the effects of conditioning generalize, so also do the effects of extinction. In reference to the example of stimulus generalization, if the 1000-cycle tone (CS) is sounded repeatedly in the absence of shock, then the conditioned fear response will extinguish. On presenting the 800- and 1200-cycle tones, following extinction of the 1000-cycle tone, we would find that their power to elicit fear had also diminished. This phenomenon is known as the *generalization of extinction.* In the example of the woman with a phobic reaction to elevators, if contingencies were arranged so that her emotional reaction to elevators was extinguished, then it would be predicted that her fear of cubicles similar to elevators, such as closets, would also be reduced. In the following case, involving the elimination of a somewhat unusual phobia, we can see the direct effect of extinction, as well as the economy associated with the generalization of extinction.

"Stardust" and the Extinction of a Music Phobia

A few years ago a young man was incapacitated because of the very intense misery he experienced whenever he heard the tune "Stardust" or tunes which reminded him of "Stardust." His life was further complicated by the fact that music in general made him distraught and uncomfortable. This phobia was so upsetting that it began to interfere with many of his daily activities. If he was in a restaurant, he had to leave if someone played the jukebox. If he was at a gathering where music was part of the entertainment, the overwhelming anxiety elicited by the music led him to escape from the situation in order to reduce his discomfort. Since music was part of nearly all of his pre-phobic routine, this unfortunate individual soon found himself withdrawing from all social activity. In desperation, he sought professional help.

Within the behavior modification orientation held by the psychologists he visited, the music phobia could be analyzed as follows: Fear of music is not an innate response. People are not born with such a fear, nor is this sort of reaction part of anyone's developmental or maturational pattern. Therefore, this reaction must have been learned. If it was learned, it must have been learned in accordance with either respondent or operant principles of conditioning. Since fear is an autonomic, emotional response, respondent conditioning was probably involved in this instance. If respondent conditioning was involved in the establishment of this music phobia, an efficient tactic in its elimination would be extinction; that is, if music (presumably a CS) is presented to the patient over and over again, the fear (CR) should abate and eventually disappear.

Notice that this analysis did not include any interpretation of the specific cause of the phobic reaction. It was assumed only that "Stardust" had become a CS for eliciting fear (it caused the most intense anxiety), and that it had at some time been paired with something the patient had experienced as unusually aversive. Then, gradually, through stimulus generalization, all music became aversive. Perhaps the precise event which occasioned this rather unusual instance of emotional conditioning could have been isolated through interviews. However, the specification of the event was of no importance to the efficacy of the extinction procedure the psychologists had selected. Extinction can be accomplished without reference to the UCS upon which the CR is based.

Notice also, that no reference was made to any internal event as a cause of the patient's dilemma. No hypotheses were proffered regarding either the patient's thoughts or the symbolic representation that "Stardust" might hold for him. The analysis was based entirely on observable events, and the therapeutic procedure was based on an objective, external, operationally defined variable: the extinction of a conditioned emotional reaction as a function of the repeated presentation of a conditioned stimulus.

Beginning with the second interview, the patient was seated in a room, and a taped version of "Stardust" and tunes the patient identified as similar to "Stardust" were played over and over again. During this session the patient evidenced all the responses characteristic of acute fear and anxiety, such as hyperventilation, sweating, and vocalizations suggesting excessive discomfort. In the third and fourth sessions, the anxiety responses were still manifest, but they were diminishing in both frequency and intensity. After a few more sessions, all of the patient's unsettling emotional reactions to music disappeared, and he appeared calm and relaxed. Tests were conducted to determine whether extinction had generalized to music unrelated to "Stardust" and to extra-therapeutic situations. According to the tests and the verbal report of the patient, this extinction procedure proved successful in the elimination of his music phobia, and he was able to resume normal activity.

The simple extinction technique employed in this case has a great deal in common with the therapy developed and named by Thomas G. Stampfl, which we will examine in the next section. His approach, while a bit more complex than the example just given, is based on the principle of respondent extinction.

Implosive Therapy: Rationale and Method

In a recent article Stampfl and Levis (1967) detailed the primary characteristics of a form of behavior therapy called implosion. In order to expedite an appreciation of this technique and the rationale which supports it, we will begin by quoting from this article. The authors wrote:

The fundamental hypothesis is that a sufficient condition for the extinction of anxiety is to re-present, reinstate, or symbolically reproduce the stimuli (cues) to which the anxiety response has been conditioned, in the absence of primary reinforcement. In a controlled laboratory situation where naive subhuman animals serve as *S*s (subjects), the above objective presents little challenge to the *E* (experimenter). In the case of the human patient, however, the contingencies of the conditioning history usually are unknown. The therapist, in his attempt to restructure the conditioning paradigms, is forced to rely mainly upon verbal reports. Considerable time is needed in treatment before sufficient information is available for the reconstruction of the important contingencies. Moreover, the accuracy of the reconstruction is questionable. Thus, at first glance, it would appear that the task of using an extinction procedure is infeasible for a short-term therapeutic approach.

Nevertheless, despite the apparent difficulty of determining the conditioning paradigms, most trained therapists, after only a few diagnostic interviews, usually find themselves speculating upon the etiology of the patient's present pathology; that is, a "good guess" about the significant personal, environmental, and dynamic interactions shaping the patient's behavior often can be made within a relatively short time. In many cases, as therapy progresses, these hypotheses are supported by the verbal report of the patient. Although these initial hypotheses are conceived only as approximations of the original conditioning paradigm, it is quite conceivable that they incorporate a number of the more significant CS components. Unfortunately, these cues are not presented systematically by the therapist using conventional techniques until he believes the patient is ready to accept them in the form of an interpretation.

However, in the implosive procedure, the emphasis is not upon the acceptance of interpretations, but rather upon the extinction of anxiety-evoking conditioned stimuli (cues) which provide both motivational and reinforcing properties for perpetuating the patient's symptoms (avoidance responses). It would also follow from the learning model that it would be irrelevant whether or not the patient "understood" or "accepted" the significance of these cues. All that is necessary for effective treatment is to represent these conditioned cues in the absence of primary reinforcement. Since the task of accurately establishing the original conditioning cues is difficult, the presentation of hypothesized cues serves as an excellent substitute. Complete accuracy is not essential since some effect, through the principle of generalization of extinction, would be expected when an approximation is presented. The more accurate the hypothesized cues and the more realistically they are presented, the greater the extinction effect would be.

The above analysis is essentially the strategy employed by implosive therapists. Hypotheses are developed about the important cues involved, and these are presented to the patient in the most vivid or realistic manner possible. Because many of the cues presented are believed originally to involve not only auditory but also visual and tactual modalities, an attempt to produce the cues in the patient's imagery, rather than a simple verbal reproduction, seems worthwhile.

The selection of hypotheses can be determined operationally by the therapist. If the cues selected elicit anxiety, the assumption is that the patient has been conditioned to them previously. The greater the degree of anxiety elicited, the greater the reason for continuing the presentations of anxiety-eliciting stimuli. To define the anxiety response, either psychophysiological techniques (e.g., GSR, heart rate) or behavioral observation (e.g., sweating, flushing of the face, increased motor behavior) can be used. In the majority of the cases, for clinical purposes, the latter method is both quite adequate and easily observable. Experience indicates that there is little difficulty in determining whether the patient is anxious. If the hypothesis presented is not confirmed by the patient's reactions, a new hypothesis is selected.

This account of the rationale of implosion is somewhat formal and concise. Nevertheless, the attentive reader should have gathered that the essential point of the quote may be reduced to one fundamental principle: If a conditioned stimulus is presented without an accompanying unconditioned stimulus (or, as Stampfl and Levis call it, an accompanying primary reinforcement), an intense emotional reaction will be generated; and, with repeated presentations of these anxiety-eliciting stimuli, the reaction will subside and cease altogether.

In regard to method, Stampfl and Levis (1967) stated that the first objective of implosive therapy is to have the patient imagine and verbalize important symptom-contingent cues. Such cues would be the conditioned stimuli that the therapist has surmised or ascertained are part of the patient's phobia, and they are selected from the real-life experiences of the patient. They include objects and situations of known "high-anxiety-eliciting-value," as determined through interview, case history, or empirical test. Prior to presenting these stimuli, the therapist establishes an *avoidance serial cue hierarchy* (ASCH). This is simply a ranking of those cues associated with a particular phobia, or phobic theme. A cue low on the hierarchy (selected, nonetheless, to elicit a great deal of anxiety) is first presented to the patient. Then, as the theme to this and related cues is "worked through" and extinguished, cues thought to be higher on the ASCH are introduced. This method is continued, and cues still higher on the ASCH are given to the patient until all areas or themes connected to the fear reaction are worked through and extinguished. This is implosive therapy as its originator viewed it. With this as background, let us review the literature bearing on this technique.

Survey of the Research

One of the first experimental reports on the application of implosive therapy (Hogan & Kirchner, 1967) dealt with the elimination of a fear of rats.

The subjects were coeds at Illinois State University who, in a pre-experiment test, refused to pick up a white rat. These "rat-phobic" subjects were then divided into an experimental group and a control group. Both groups were then given a therapy session which averaged a little more than one-half hour. In the therapy session, each subject of the experimental group was asked to engage in imagery pertaining to rats. This imagery began with mild scenes of the subject touching a rat or of a rat nibbling at the subject's finger. Later, intensely emotional scenes were suggested—including scenes of the rodent piercing the subject viciously in the neck, climbing into her mouth, and destroying various internal organs. Although all experimental subjects were required to imagine rat scenes, the scenes were modified with each individual to increase the probability that intense anxiety would be generated. In contrast, control subjects were asked to imagine scenes divorced from the rat theme, such as taking a leisurely walk or enjoying a relaxed vacation.

After therapy all subjects were given a post-test opportunity to pick up a white rat, which might be regarded as the primary criterion for the elimination of the relevant phobia. Fourteen of the twenty-one experimental subjects proceeded to the rat and picked it up, while twenty of the twenty-two control subjects still refused to lift the rodent. The authors concluded that short-term implosive therapy effectively changed the experimental group's behavior; that the minimal amount of time required for the extinction of the fear augmented the value of the implosive technique; and that the implosive idea—that is, of having subjects experience anxiety in the absence of primary reinforcement (the UCS) in order to extinguish fear—was supported by the experiment.

Another study (Hogan, 1966) reported on the application of implosion in the treatment of psychotics. Patients in a state hospital were divided into two groups of approximately twenty-five subjects each. The subjects of the experimental group were treated by implosion, and the others were given traditional therapy. Patient improvement was assessed immediately after treatment as well as in a follow-up one year later. The group given implosive therapy displayed significant shifts away from psychopathology as measured by the Minnesota Multiphasic Personality Inventory. The experimental group also indicated more success than the control group when release from the hospital was used as a criterion of success.

A similar study, by Levis and Carrera (1967), was designed to investigate the effectiveness of implosive therapy with outpatients, as well as to test the feasibility of broader evaluations of implosion. Forty patients were divided into four groups. Besides the experimental (IT) group, whose members received ten hours of implosive therapy, there was a control group which received ten hours of conventional insight and supportive therapy; a second control group, which received an average of thirty-seven hours of conventional therapy; and a third control group, which was composed of nontreated patients. Patient improvement was assessed by a pre-test and post-test administration of the Minnesota Multiphasic Personality Inventory. Based on the results of this inventory, the investigators concluded that there was a consistent trend for the IT group away from psychopathology, while no such trend was apparent for patients in the control groups. However, the authors did point out that some sort of "placebo effect" may have biased the data in "favor" of the IT group, since it employed a rather new and different technique. The need for more extensive research, in order to delineate more clearly the efficacy of implosion, was emphasized.

Concluding Comments

Implosive therapists believe that their technique is applicable and appropriate to the treatment of a variety of behavior problems. Among the problems they mention are anxiety, as well as phobic, obsessive-compulsive, and depressive reactions. They point out that this technique has also been applied successfully to psychotic disorders including affective, schizophrenic, and paranoid reactions, and that it also holds promise in the treatment of personality disorders including homosexuality, alcoholism, and speech disturbances. Assuming that these claims may gain empirical support, one of the major contributions of implosion will be the relatively short time required for therapeutic progress. Proponents of implosion have stated that marked changes in symptomatology are achieved in from one to fifteen one-hour sessions, with total treatment time rarely exceeding thirty implosive hours. If increased empirical support is forthcoming, and if the empirical basis is more firmly established in research, this approach should prove beneficial to innumerable people—especially people who cannot afford therapy of long duration.

Selected Readings

Implosive therapy is of very recent origin, and studies pertinent to this approach are few in number. In fact, it is believed that all of the available research on implosion was covered in our survey in this chapter. Consequently, little can be added for the reader in the way of supplemental readings at this time. It should be noted, however, that exponents of this therapeutic orientation are actively engaged in research—as evidenced through personal communications and formal notices of pending meetings. It is highly probable, therefore, that the serious student may uncover new research and developments in implosion by reviewing the relevant psychological journals. The journals which are most likely to carry articles in this area in the near future are the following:

Behaviour Research and Therapy

Journal of Abnormal Psychology

Journal of Consulting and Clinical Psychology

Psychotherapy: Theory, Research, and Practice

3 Modification of Respondent Behavior: Desensitization

Counterconditioning

In autonomic, respondent emotional reactions, there are certain responses which do not "go together," which are incompatible; if one occurs, the other is precluded, and vice versa. One cannot experience intense hate and love, or excitement and tranquillity, at the same time. Nor can one be anxious and relaxed in any given moment, since the two responses are opposite, incompatible emotional reactions. Various behavior modification techniques use the concept of the incompatible response in the treatment of autonomic, conditioned emotional reactions; and at the root of these various treatments is a process called *counterconditioning*. Counterconditioning is the process whereby a new CR, which is incompatible with the CR to be eliminated, is conditioned to the CS. If counterconditioning has been effected, the presentation of the CS will elicit the new CR rather than the original CR.

We can clarify the dynamics of the counterconditioning process by considering a series of paradigms. Suppose, first, that we pair a 1000-cycle tone with an electric shock (Step 1) so that, after a few such associations have been presented to a subject, the tone itself comes to elicit an emotional reaction similar to that elicited by the shock (Step 2).

(1) CS (1000-cycle tone)
          ↓
      (paired with)
          ↓
UCS (shock) → elicits → UCR (fear)

(2) CS (1000-cycle tone) → elicits → CR (fear)

Assuming that we have decided to eliminate fear as a conditioned response to the 1000-cycle tone through counterconditioning, we must first select a response that is incompatible with fear. A reasonable selection might be the response of salivation and the related "pleasurable" responses associated with eating. We would begin by choosing a tone sufficiently dissimilar to the 1000-cycle tone (perhaps a 500-cycle tone) and pairing it with food presentation (Step 3) when our subject was very hungry. By using a dissimilar tone, we would reduce the probability that it would elicit strong fear and increase our chances of establishing a new reaction to the tone. If our stimulus selection proved to be judicious, we would then have a new conditioned response (Step 4).

(3) CS (500-cycle tone)
          ↓
      (paired with)
          ↓
UCS (food) → elicits → UCR (salivation)

(4) CS (500-cycle tone) → elicits → CR (salivation)

The stimulus selected in Step 3 is crucial. If it is too similar to the original CS (1000-cycle tone), we would produce excessive fear, thereby impeding the counterconditioning attempt or perhaps obviating it altogether. A second problem would be the selection of a stimulus so dissimilar to the original CS that counterconditioning would not be promoted. Let us imagine, however, that our selection was wise, and that the minimal fear elicited by the 500-cycle tone was weaker than the contrasting emotions associated with "food-in-the-mouth" of a hungry person. If this was the case, then the new conditioned respondent, as given in Step 4, will have been established. This brings us to the concept of *hierarchies* in counterconditioning technique.

Since the ultimate goal in our example is to present a 1000-cycle tone which will elicit salivation rather than fear, we must gradually increase the pitch of the tone selected to initiate counterconditioning until it reaches 1000 cycles. Two processes are at work here. Each time we are able to present the CS and to have it followed by salivation, a new stimulus-response connection is being formed, and the original connection is being extinguished. However, if we approximate the original CS too rapidly, we run the danger of eliciting fear rather than salivation. Consequently, we construct a hierarchy of CSs, beginning with those least like the original CS, and gradually increase the similarity until we finally employ the 1000-cycle tone itself. Each approximation to the original CS strengthens the new CS-salivation connection, since we continue to pair the CS with the UCS, food. Further, each approximation decreases the CS-fear connection, through extinction, since we never pair the CS with the UCS, shock. As mentioned, if our hierarchy has been properly planned, the combined forces of reconditioning and extinction at each step will eventually result in the elicitation of salivation (in place of fear) when the original 1000-cycle tone is presented. Let us now consider an early clinical application of counterconditioning.

Children's Fears: A Prototype of Counterconditioning

Jones (1924), who was working with children's fears and phobias, developed a counterconditioning technique which was efficient, practical, and effective. She had decided to use "feeding" and the feeding situation as a means of helping her young patients overcome their anxieties. She describes her approach as follows:

> During a period of craving for food, the child is placed in a high chair and given something to eat. The feared object is brought in, starting a negative response. It is then moved away gradually until it is at a sufficient distance not to interfere with the child's eating. The relative strength of the fear impulse and the hunger impulse may be gauged by the distance to which it is necessary to remove the feared object. While the child is eating, the object is slowly brought nearer to the table, then placed upon the table, and finally as the tolerance increases it is brought close enough to be touched. Since we could not interfere with the regular schedule of meals, we chose the time of the mid-morning lunch for the experiment. This usually assured some degree of interest in the food and corresponding success in our experiment (1924).

In this account a "food-craved" child is given something to eat (eating is a response incompatible with fear). A feared object (CS) is then brought in, and a negative response occurs (CR fear). The feared object is then moved away so as not to interfere with eating, but it remains in the same room. If the child now continues to eat, the original stimulus-response connection is being partly extinguished, and the new connection is begun. In essence, this case is similar to what we described in Step 4 of our counterconditioning paradigm. While the child is eating, the feared object is brought nearer and nearer to his table. This could be isolated into a series composing a hierarchy such as the one we used with tones. But the similarity or dissimilarity of the CS in Jones's example would be gauged by distance rather than cycles per second. As the object is brought into closer proximity, the dual processes of extinction and reconditioning are in effect. Finally, the child holds and plays with the object that formerly elicited fear, and he continues to "munch" food enthusiastically. Counterconditioning has been accomplished. If the child were handed the object at some later date, he should show no fear; rather, the autonomic responses which characterize eating would more likely be in evidence.

With this background, we are now ready to make a thorough appraisal of one of the best-established and most widely used counterconditioning techniques: systematic desensitization.

Reciprocal Inhibition: Rationale and Method

As developed by Wolpe in his first book (1958) and reworked later in other texts (Wolpe & Lazarus, 1966; Wolpe, 1969), *reciprocal inhibition* is a generic term for those behavior therapies which rely on a variety of techniques employing counterconditioning. Among these techniques are assertive training, the substitution of sexual responses for anxiety responses, and systematic desensitization. We will concern ourselves only with the latter, since, of all the behavior therapies, systematic desensitization has one of the broadest empirical bases. It is the most widely used technique among behavior therapists; and, most importantly for our purposes, it is directed specifically to respondent modification and is well aligned with our account of counterconditioning

The heart of Wolpe's approach is what he has called the "reciprocal inhibition principle," a principle that we attempted to develop in our sections on Counterconditioning and Children's Fears. The principle, as written by Wolpe and Lazarus (1966), is this: "If a response inhibitory of anxiety can be made to occur in the presence of anxiety-evoking stimuli, it will weaken the bond between these stimuli and the anxiety (p. 12)." In systematic desensitization the "response inhibitory of anxiety" is complete relaxation, and the "anxiety-evoking stimuli" are the fears and phobias which the patient brings to the clinic. The elimination of these fears and phobias through extinction, and the reconditioning of former anxiety-stimuli to the responses associated with complete relaxation, constitute the process of systematic desensitization. As outlined by Wolpe, this process involves three operations: (1) training in deep muscle relaxation; (2) the construction of anxiety hierarchies; and (3) counterposing relaxation and anxiety-evoking stimuli from the hierarchies.

The first of these operations is similar to the method of relaxation developed by Jacobson (1938), and with Wolpe's modifications it requires only a few interviews for its completion. The patient is first instructed regarding the nature of complete relaxation, after which he is given progressive relaxation training of various parts of his body until complete relaxation is achieved. To appreciate the technique more fully, we will take a brief look at how Wolpe would proceed with relaxation training of one of the major muscle groups, the arms. After the patient has assumed a comfortable position, he is then told (Wolpe, 1969):

> I am now going to show you the essential activity that is involved in obtaining deep relaxation. I shall again ask you to resist my pull at your wrist so as to tighten your biceps. I want you to notice very carefully the sensations in that muscle. Then I shall ask you to let go gradually as I diminish the amount of force exerted against you. Notice, as your forearm descends, that there is decreasing sensation in the biceps muscle. Notice also that the letting go is an activity, but of a negative kind—it is an 'uncontracting' of the muscle. In due course, your forearm will come to rest on the arm of the chair, and you may then think that you have gone as far as possible—that relaxation is complete. But although the biceps will indeed be partly and perhaps largely relaxed, a certain number of its fibers will still, in fact, be contracted. I shall therefore say to you, 'Go on letting go. Try to extend the activity that went on in the biceps while your forearm was coming down.' It is the act of relaxing these additional fibers that will bring about the emotional effects we want. Let's try it and see what happens (p. 102).

This general program is then continued through the major muscle groups. Besides receiving training in the therapeutic session, the patient is also directed to practice the technique by himself a couple of times daily, so that when the course is completed he will be able to relax his entire body in a few seconds.

One of the most difficult aspects of systematic desensitization is the construction of anxiety hierarchies, a task which in many cases requires considerable ingenuity on the part of the therapist. The function of the hierarchy, as we saw in our account of counterconditioning, is to extinguish the fear response and to recondition relaxation responses to the stimuli which elicit anxiety. Wolpe's rationale and assumptions pertaining to the hierarchy are clearly given in his text as follows (1969):

> Once a weak stimulus has ceased to arouse any anxiety, it is possible to present a somewhat stronger stimulus to the fully relaxed patient and this stronger stimulus will now evoke less anxiety than it would have done before. Successive presentations will bring the amount of anxiety aroused down to zero. Stronger and stronger stimuli are thus brought within the anxiety-inhibiting capacity of the subject's relaxation. To put the matter in another way, if there are ten stimuli which in their variations along a single dimension

evoke in a subject quantities of anxiety which vary from one to ten, and if through the inhibiting effects of relaxation the anxiety aroused by the stimulus evoking one unit is reduced to zero, the stimulus originally evoking two units of anxiety will be found to be evoking only one unit. . . Thus, in an acrophobic subject who has one unit of anxiety produced by looking out of a second floor window and two units by looking out of a third floor window, reduction of the amount of anxiety from the second floor window to zero would have the effect that the amount of anxiety evoked at a third floor window would be diminished to one unit. It must be emphasized that these decrements of response are not transient but lasting. As in the animal experiments they are indicative of decrease of strength of anxiety-response habits (pp. 97-98).

The importance of proper hierarchy construction should be obvious. The material must be related to the phobia, and the items must begin at a point tangential to the phobia. To move at too rapid a pace, or to initially present items which are too closely related to the phobia, would produce an anxiety reaction, disturb the patient's relaxed state, and thereby impede therapeutic progress.

Content for the anxiety hierarchies is obtained from a patient's history, an "interpersonal" anxiety scale, a fear survey, and clinical probings into the situations which the patient finds fearful. When all the areas of disturbance have been listed, they are classified into themes. A theme is then broken into specific statements about the theme, and these statements are ranked in ascending order according to the degree of anxiety they elicit. With the patient able to relax himself satisfactorily, and with the anxiety hierarchies constructed, the desensitization procedure is begun.

The patient is asked to relax. When this is complete he is told that he will soon be asked to imagine various scenes, and that if he becomes slightly anxious at any time, he is to raise his index finger. If a scene low on the anxiety hierarchy is presented for imagery and the patient indicates no anxiety (which suggests the converse, that he is relaxed and serene), then another scene just one step higher on the hierarchy is presented. This is continued until all the scenes of the hierarchy have been imagined by the patient. If at any time the patient indicates anxiety, however, the therapist retreats to an earlier scene which did not elicit discomfort and slowly works back up the hierarchy. The manner in which scenes are introduced is nicely demonstrated by the case of Miss C. (Wolpe, 1969). When the patient was relaxed, the therapist began:

> I am now going to ask you to imagine a number of scenes. You will imagine them clearly and they will generally interfere little, if at all, with your state of relaxation. If, however, at any time you feel disturbed or worried and want to draw my attention, you will be

able to do so by raising your left index finger. First I want you to imagine that you are standing at a familiar street corner on a pleasant morning watching the traffic go by. You see cars, motorcycles, trucks, bicycles, people and traffic lights; and you can hear the sounds associated with all these things. (Pause of about 15 sec.) Now stop imagining that scene and give all your attention once again to relaxing. If the scene you imagine disturbed you even in the slightest degree I want you to raise your left index finger *now*. (Patient does not raise finger.) Now imagine that you are home studying in the evening. It is the 20th of May, exactly a month before your examination. (Pause of 5 sec.) Now stop imagining the scene. Go on relaxing. (Pause of 5 sec.) Now imagine the same scene again—a month before your examination. (Pause of 5 sec.) Stop imagining the scene and just think of your muscles. Let go, and enjoy your state of calm. (Pause of 15 sec.) Now again imagine that you are studying at home a month before your examination. (Pause of 5 sec.) Stop the scene, and now think of nothing but your own body. (Pause of 5 sec.) If you felt any disturbance whatsoever to the last scene raise your left index finger now. (Patient raises finger.) If the amount of disturbance decreased from the first presentation to the third do nothing, otherwise again raise your finger. (Patient raises finger.) If the amount of disturbance decreased from the first presentation to the third do nothing, otherwise again raise your finger. (Patient does not raise finger.) Just keep on relaxing. (Pause of 15 sec.) Imagine that you are sitting on a bench at a bus stop and across the road are two strange men whose voices are raised in argument. (Pause of 10 sec.) Stop imagining the scene and just relax. (Pause of 10 sec.) Now again imagine the scene of these two men arguing across the road. (Pause of 10 sec.) Stop the scene and relax. Now I am going to count up to 5 and you will open your eyes, feeling very calm and refreshed (pp. 126-127).

When all the items of a hierarchy have been presented to the patient, and all hierarchies pertaining to the patient's emotional disturbances have been covered in the absence of anxiety, counterconditioning should be complete. The primary criterion of success in the therapeutic endeavor is whether the patient can now comfortably confront those situations which, in the past, caused him distress. With this in mind, we will now review some of the literature in which this form of reciprocal inhibition has been applied.

Survey of Research and Case Histories

The variety of respondent disturbances successfully ameliorated by systematic desensitization is very broad. Among those treated and reported by Wolpe and Lazarus (1966) are fears and anxieties related to closed places, height, illness, storms, guilt, examinations, being watched, jealousy, crowds, criticism, personal devaluation, palpitations, talking before an audience, authority figures, falling, death, rejection, masturbation, disapproval, failing, stuttering, and sex. These authors also report that the time required for this technique is very economical, with a mean number of sessions per phobia of 11.2, which is in sharp contrast with traditional therapies—particularly analytically oriented therapies.

As a first example, we will consider the case of the patient who was terrified by a persistent, recurrent nightmare (Geer & Silverman, 1967). Here the therapist planned what we would consider a well-derived and straightforward counterconditioning strategy. He simply constructed a hierarchy with the nightmare as the central theme and presented this hierarchy to the patient under conditions of extreme relaxation. After only a few sessions the nightmare disappeared, and a follow-up study showed that it had never recurred. In light of traditional therapeutic approaches to similar problems, these results were dramatic.

Another study reported on the treatment of a patient, a young man, who had formed a post-traumatic phobia following a car accident (Kushner, 1966). Prior to the accident, the patient had a consuming interest in autos; afterward, however, he found that he was anxious around cars, uneasy in cars driven by others, and unable to drive his own car. The inability to drive his own car was particularly distressing to the young man, reflecting the intensity of his fears. This impasse was also reflected in other ways: He was tense and anxious, and he had a poor appetite and a great deal of difficulty in falling asleep; further, he was generally more grouchy and irritable, and he noted a decrease in his ability to concentrate. Desensitization was selected as the means of reducing the patient's high anxiety level and phobic reactions.

In the first session the patient was given instruction in how to achieve deep relaxation. When next seen, the patient was given additional practice in progressive relaxation, and desensitization was begun. He was first required to imagine looking at his car, and then to imagine leaning against it; and this session terminated with the patient visualizing himself sitting in the car.

In subsequent sessions the hierarchy included sitting in the car, turning the ignition on, allowing the car to idle motionless, then backing the car out of the driveway, driving around the block, and approaching an intersection. At this point the patient indicated some anxiety, and he was then told to "erase" the scene and to concentrate on relaxing. In the fourth session the patient's tasks were to imagine the following scenes: driving along a road with no intersections; approaching an intersection with no traffic; and then approaching the same intersection with another car approaching from the right, where there was a "Stop" sign. This last scene was rather "high" in the hierarchy, because it approximated the actual accident which precipitated the patient's difficulties. Since mild anxiety was elicited, this entire series was repeated, and the patient remained completely relaxed during the second "run."

By the fifth session the young man reported that he had improved considerably and that he was driving his car. He appeared more relaxed, and he was generally more responsive, spontaneous, alert, and happy. Desensitization was continued, employing scenes involving traffic, intersections, and reconstructions of the accident itself. No anxiety was elicited. The case was concluded at the next meeting. As Kushner reported (1965):

> The sixth and final session was held two and one-half weeks following the first contact with the patient. At this time the patient considered himself ninety percent better. He had no trouble sleeping at night, his appetite was normal, he was no longer irritable, and his concentration in school had improved considerably. Relaxation techniques were reinforced at this last session and he was instructed in the various ways that he could bring these to bear and thus make his everyday activities more effective. The patient was discharged and a three months follow-up revealed still further improvement with no exacerbation of his earlier symptoms (p.195).

In another very interesting case, pseudonecrophilia was treated by behavior therapy (Lazarus, 1968). The patient was fearful of the opposite sex, and described himself as terrified at the prospect of engaging a "real live woman" sexually. Rather, his sex life was limited to masturbation, accompanied by fantasies of "always beautiful, always dead" women. His general distress and guilt over this sexual practice brought him to a clinic. As in the preceding case, the therapist's approach was direct, the aim being to eliminate the patient's fear of women and to induce more acceptable heterosexual experiences.

After the patient had been trained to achieve deep relaxation, he was asked to imagine scenes from a heterosexual hierarchy. He was first told to imagine himself being sexually aroused by and in front of a dead woman. When the patient could imagine this scene without anxiety, the therapist introduced the next scene, which required the patient to imagine being aroused by an unconscious woman. The next step in the hierarchy involved imaginary sexual contact with an anesthetized woman, and then with a woman who had passed out after having too much to drink. Succeeding steps depicted the patient having intercourse with a semiconscious woman who would remember nothing when she regained consciousness, and then with a prostitute whose attention was diverted.

The results were very encouraging, and the patient reported having had intercourse with a girl friend after the fifth desensitization session. As therapy continued (a total of 17 sessions), the patient's heterosexual interests increased. There was also an associated improvement in other aspects of his social behavior, and he appeared content and well adjusted. In a letter to the therapist, eleven months after the termination of therapy, the patient indicated that all was well.

4 The versatility of systematic desensitization was illustrated in a study by Cowden and Ford (1962), who treated two patients who had been diagnosed as "schizophrenic reaction, paranoid type." Both patients had also shown clear-cut phobic behavior. One patient, whose case we will consider here, was a 27-year-old male who had begun to manifest withdrawal "symptoms" while in the Marine Corps. On returning home he became very restless and tense, he refused to work, and he drank excessively. Later he began to hallucinate, and he developed delusions of reference, influence, and persecution. He was admitted to a "mental" hospital, but various drugs and traditional psychotherapies proved to be of little value. One of this patient's more outstanding interpersonal difficulties was his inability to talk to other people without becoming extremely panicky and frightened. Because of this phobic reaction, the authors felt that he might profit from systematic desensitization.

After the patient had been trained in progressive relaxation, Cowden and Ford constructed a hierarchy in which the patient was to imagine himself "talking freely" in various situations. Some of the items in the hierarchy, which was presented over a series of eighteen therapeutic sessions, are listed below. The patient was to imagine talking freely:

> About a movie you saw.
>
> About your experience to an interested and sympathetic nurse.
>
> About something extremely serious in a joking manner to nurse B.
>
> To a patient in the canteen who looks sloppy or revolting to you.
>
> About current events to someone you consider less intelligent than you.
>
> About current events to someone you consider more intelligent than you.
>
> About your symptoms of mental illness to your therapist.
>
> About your symptoms of mental illness to the ward nurse, Miss B. or Miss D.
>
> About your personal difficulties to a pretty girl in a restaurant.
>
> About your symptoms of mental illness and very personal difficulties to Dr. E.
>
> About your very personal difficulties to your sister.

In view of (a) the singularly unsuccessful consequences of other methods of treatment and (b) the relatively short period of counterconditioning therapy, the results of systematic desensitization were dramatic. As Cowden and Ford reported:

> When about half way through the hierarchy, the patient, ward personnel, and others who worked with the patient reported that he was more relaxed, friendly, and much more talkative. Auditory hallucinations had ceased before the experiment. However, there were other symptoms which bothered him and these began to decrease in severity. They ceased entirely within a month or two after the last experimental session. These were unusual thoughts, vivid dreams which disturbed his sleep, and ideas of reference. He began going home on passes again. He became regular in attendance and efficient in his work assignments. Cigarette smoking decreased. In regular therapy he talked freely and at length and was able to discuss things he had not mentioned in more than 3 years.
>
> Patient reported that he still had some difficulty in talking in a very talkative group. For example, once while home on a weekend, many relatives were there and everyone seemed to be trying to talk at the same time. Patient stated he felt overwhelmed and had to leave the room.
>
> However, on a pass in early May he discussed with his mother and father the possibility of his coming home to live with them when discharged from the hospital. This was a very unusual bit of behavior for this patient. However, the parents refused to accept him at home. He stated that he felt very disappointed and was somewhat depressed afterwards. So far, no adverse effects have become manifest, and the patient continues to be relatively talkative. This case might well be considered a successful demonstration of desensitization therapy with schizophrenic subjects (1962).

Another aspect of the preceding case is relevant at this point, because it underscores a basic distinction between behavior therapies and other methods of therapy. Cowden and Ford noted that "in many instances a patient is confined to a mental hospital because of one primary phobic or obsessional symptom. In some cases, if this symptom can be removed, the patient could return to society." Why, in this particular instance, was the person not returned to his home? A good guess is that his parents made an error that is also made by many professional personnel: namely, the error of reification. The noun becomes the cause. On the basis of his behavior he was given a label—"schizophrenic reaction, paranoid type"—which, in the eyes of the patient's family and the hospital attendants, became a *cause* rather than a summary description of his behavior. What was clearly wrong with the patient was his *behavior*. His behavior was what led to abrasive interpersonal relationships and eventually to hospitalization. But, even with the behavior modified into more acceptable patterns, the fallacy—he is a "schizophrenic"—probably prevailed; thus, the patient remained hospitalized. While behavior modification techniques are being used with resounding success in the treatment of patients, the persistence of such fallacies—among both professionals and laymen—remains a problem.

An interesting application of the counterconditioning model was reported by Wilson and Smith (1968) in their study of diffuse, non-specific anxiety (pan-anxiety). In contrast to the typical desensitization preliminaries in which the therapist constructs a hierarchy, the procedure in this case involved the patient's use of the "free-association" technique as a means of building and working on one or more anxiety hierarchies in each session. Wilson and Smith hypothesized "that free association, used in conjunction with muscle relaxation, would be an efficient means simultaneously to define and to countercondition complexes of anxiety-mediating stimuli." The therapists assumed that the patient's associations would begin with stimuli somewhat distant from the anxiety foci, and that deconditioning of anxiety to these distant associations would generalize to the more important stimuli. Further, as extinction generalized, the patient would be able to move closer and closer to the anxiety foci as therapy progressed.

In order to see how this free-association technique was applied, let us consider some of the details of the case of Mr. B., as reported by Wilson and Smith (1968):

> Mr. B, 40 yr. old, had divorced his first wife on grounds of adultery and married her younger sister. The family relationships were extremely conflict laden. The first wife still lived close by and was reported to be interfering constantly in the affairs of his present family. A teen-aged daughter's acting out posed a special problem. The family was being supported by public welfare. The tenor of the family relationships was one of bitter hostility. Further, the patient was dissatisfied with his work; although his work record was good while on the job, he would typically be overly passive toward his employer, allowing himself to be abused until he became so overwhelmingly resentful, depressed, and anxious that he could not continue on the job. Mr. B. was admitted to the hospital complaining of dissociative episodes during which he would sometimes physically attack strangers on the street, fainting spells, constant irritability, muscle spasms, and stomach cramps. After entering the hospital he developed a duodenal ulcer with considerable attendant weight loss. Although he was seeing a hospital staff psychiatrist regularly for therapy interviews, and was taking tranquilizing drugs, his condition steadily worsened. The psychologist who tested him felt that "it would require a long period before a 'working' or therapeutic transference could be established with him." The authors first saw Mr. B. about 5 mos. after his admission.

Method

A diagnostic interview was conducted focusing on the history of the patient's symptoms and interpersonal problems. It seemed that this patient's trouble was the inability to make appropriate and well-modulated assertive responses because of intense anxiety and a consequent chronic angry submission to others. A treatment sequence was planned of, first, counterconditioning of anxiety responses; second, advice and support in making appropriate assertive responses; and finally, if necessary, family therapy.

Counterconditioning

The patient lay comfortably on a couch. Surface EMG electrodes were attached to the trapezius group, which proved adequately reactive to interview content. The patient was taught muscle relaxation. . . A light to moderate hypnotic trance was induced subsequent to relaxation by the eye-fixation method. A suggestion was given to the patient that, as he thought of things related to his problems, his mind would become very clear, and he would see all that he talked about quite clearly. It was emphasized that no matter what he talked about, he would remain calm and relaxed. No other suggestions were given. The patient reported that the relaxed trance state was very pleasant, and that he experienced vivid visual imagery, "just like being there," in the situations he described. That this was true can be inferred from the readily apparent rapid eye movements that accompanied his descriptions. If a particular associational sequence led to considerable muscle tension on the EMG display for more than 5-10 sec., the therapist would ask the patient to stop and relax, then return to the sequence until it could be handled with no observable muscle tension. This was rarely necessary; usually the patient's self-pacing was quite satisfactory. The therapist made no interpretations. His remarks were limited to an occasional reflection of the patient's feelings, or a request that the patient continue or stop and relax. That is, the therapist concerned himself primarily with the pacing of the interview.

Following is an example of the fifth session.

Therapist: Can you remember the first time you ever had a fainting spell?

Patient: . . . I was in basic training . . . we were firing a 20 millimeter gun. I was standing by the gun mount . . . it was a cold day, that's all I can remember . . . I must have passed out. I came to and I was lying by the gun mount on concrete. I was cold. My vision was bad . . . I was told to go to the first aid station . . . I sat in a chair to wait for the doctor and I passed out again in the chair . . . I drank some coffee and went to the hospital . . . My temperature was below normal, I was real cold . . . I was kept in the hospital for two days . . . I didn't like the hospital, I kept getting shots in the arms and the nurse wouldn't let me get out of bed . . . They gave me a yellow liquid that made me gag, it tasted like it had alcohol in it . . . the doctor told me I wasn't going to be able to go back . . .

Therapist: O.K. stop and relax.

Mr. B. went on to recall how dissatisfied he was with the treatment he had received and how angry he was at the doctor for "lying" to him. "He told me I'd get over this, but I still have fainting spells."

As treatment progressed the patient's association tended to become more relevant to his current problems. After 16 biweekly counter-conditioning sessions the patient was asymptomatic. The fainting, dissociation, muscle spasms, and stomach distress were gone; he had begun to gain weight slowly; his mood was much improved. A follow-up barium X-ray series showed the ulcer to be inactive and healing well. Mr. B had spontaneously begun to make more asser-tive responses, especially in handling family affairs when home on pass. It was felt, however, that he still needed more practice in this area (1968).

The case of Mr. B is but one illustration of the ingenuity which is typical of those psychologists who apply behavior modification techniques. In this instance the unique combination of "free association" and deep relaxation provided the effective counterconditioning setting which dramatically modified very "severe" maladaptive behaviors. It would appear that coun-terconditioning has some saliency whenever the therapeutic focus is on a conditioned, autonomic, emotional reaction.

Evaluation of Respondent Therapies

For the modification of adverse, conditioned emotional reactions, both implosive therapy and systematic desensitization seem to have several advantages over other, non-behavior therapies. First, and perhaps most apparent, is the fact that respondent therapies are relatively brief and economical, thus making treatment available and feasible for more people. By contrast, the more traditional therapies often extend treatment over years, thereby limiting to those who can afford them whatever benefits might accrue from such treatment.

A more significant advantage of behavior therapy over many other forms of treatment is its goal of modifying reactions that are objective as well as readily identifiable and easily measurable. This goal leads to a specifically defined criterion of therapeutic progress and success. Many non-behavior therapies speak of helping the individual actuate his potential, realize a better self-image, resolve his Oedipal complex, or put his id, ego, and superego in better harmony. Whatever these things might mean, they are completely irrelevant unless the patient's emotional reactions are less dis-tressing to him and his behavior is more adaptive.

In contrast to the traditional therapist, the psychologist who embraces the behavior modification viewpoint asks three questions when confronted with a patient seeking help: (1) What specifically is the behavior to be modified? (2) What are the stimuli currently maintaining the behavior? (3) What are the variables which will produce the appropriate behavior modification?

In all of the cases we have considered, what the therapist attempted to modify was behavior, and what he manipulated in producing a change was an external variable based on principles of respondent conditioning. This is the final plus for the behavior therapies we have covered. They have as their foundation the empirically established, easily stated principles of respondent extinction and counterconditioning. Moreover, the operational clarity of such principles lends the behavior therapy techniques to new, and more effective, variations and innovations. Even now there are researchers working on the feasibility of programmed, automated, desensitization techniques, and their efforts may be of tremendous advantage to the "would be" patients who today can only "grin and bear it."

Selected Readings

The student who is interested in systematic desensitization or other reciprocal inhibition techniques may profit from Wolpe's most recent book, which is intended to provide a statement of the fundamental principles of behavior therapy and to review recent developments in this field. In conjunction with an exposition of the theory and practice of his approach, Wolpe also offers a number of case histories designed to elucidate and demonstrate this kind of therapy.

Wolpe, J. *The practice of behavior therapy.* Elmsford, N.Y.: Pergamon, 1969.

The following book is designed to provide a comprehensive review of behavior therapy. In addition to reviewing techniques, the book gives attention to the philosophical and experimental basis of the behavior therapies, along with consideration of various social aspects and current issues.

Franks, C. M. (Ed.) *Behavior therapy: Appraisal and status.* New York: McGraw-Hill, 1969.

4

Reinforcement and the Modification of Operant Behavior

Positive Reinforcement, Conditioning, and Extinction

As we discussed in Chapter 1, operant behavior encompasses much of the ongoing, daily behavior of a person in commerce with other persons, as well as the individual's interaction with his general environment. Operants constitute what an individual *does* and *says* as he moves about promoting change in the many aspects of his immediate environment. As a man drives his car, plays with his children, works at his job, attends the theater, brings his wife flowers, and cheerfully says "good morning" to his boss, he is engaging in instances of operant responding. In the proper context, these are appropriate and adaptive operant responses.

In contrast to these adaptive responses, and of central concern to us in this text, are the operants that are maladaptive—that lead to an individual's felt discomfort and distress, or that bring a person's actions to the attention of his family and friends or, as is often the case, the authorities. Sometimes maladaptive behavior is that which antedates and precipitates commitment to any number and variety of "mental health" programs. Operants in this category would include the taking of drugs and the excessive use of alcohol, the delusions of the paranoic, and the "opposite speech" of schizophrenics. Here also would be included the milder forms of abrasion such as extreme moodiness, excessive depression or elation, and frequent "irrational" and disruptive behavior that fosters intervention by public health workers or other social agents.

In order to understand these maladaptive behaviors and the principles upon which operant modification techniques are based, let us first consider the processes by which any operant behavior—adaptive or maladaptive—is acquired and attenuated. This brings us to the law of operant conditioning, and to the most important single concept in all of operant modification: *positive reinforcement.* A positive reinforcing stimulus may be formally defined as *any stimulus which, when it follows a response, will increase the strength or maintain the occurrence of that response.* Common examples of positive reinforcing stimuli are food, water, and sex, as well as more complex stimuli such as attention, affection, and approval. Under appropriate circumstances, any operant response followed by one of these stimuli will gain in strength. When an operant response (R) is strengthened after it has been succeeded by a positive reinforcer (S^{R+}), operant conditioning has taken place. The significance and subtlety of this principle will become apparent later in the chapter when we discuss its current application to therapy. For the moment, let us refer to a simple example, and draw the basic paradigm, of operant conditioning.

Imagine that we have placed a food-deprived rat in a small experimental chamber containing a bar, or lever. Suppose further that we have arranged things in such a way that whenever the rat depresses the lever, an electrical impulse is activated, and a small pellet of food is delivered to a receptacle located in the animal's chamber. Initially, as the albino rat casually moves about his cage, he will press the lever by chance; food will then be made available, and he will eat it. After only a few lever presses (R) of this sort, followed by the consumption of food pellets (S^{R+}), his lever-pressing behavior will increase radically. The rat has then been operantly conditioned. The paradigm for this event is:

$$R - - - \rightarrow S^{R+}$$

The paradigm simply means that when the availability of food is contingent upon the rat's pressing a lever, the food will function as a positive reinforcer and will increase the operant behavior, lever pressing. Now, as long as the rat remains "hungry," and as long as food is a consequence of lever pressing, this behavior will continue to be very probable (emitted at a high frequency). The rat has thus learned a particular behavior; a particular operant response has been conditioned, because that response has been positively reinforced.

Related to operant conditioning, and directly relevant to behavior therapy, is the question of how one should proceed to eliminate a conditioned operant. The answer is uncomplicated: One eliminates a conditioned operant response by terminating the contingency between that response and the reinforcing stimulus. This is called *operant extinction*. When the response-reinforcement contingency is no longer in effect, the rate of the response gradually declines and finally ceases. The paradigm for extinction is the same as that for conditioning, except that a line is drawn through the arrow, indicating that the contingency no longer prevails.

$$R---/--\rightarrow S^{R+}$$

These two very basic paradigms, operant conditioning and operant extinction, provide the basis for the very significant and often startling results of contemporary behavior modification techniques. Before we review some of these results, however, we will first consider the concepts of operant shaping and schedules of reinforcement—concepts which also figure significantly in behavior therapy.

Shaping

In the above illustration of operant conditioning, we did not condition a new response, but simply strengthened one that was already included in the rodent's behavioral repertoire. As the rat explored the experimental chamber, it was only by chance that the bar was occasionally pressed, and the effect of conditioning was to increase the frequency of this behavior. However, through a process known as *shaping*, completely new operants can be made part of the animal's repertoire. For instance, in their search for food, rats would seldom be found "rolling over" in order to obtain their daily ration. Nevertheless, "rolling over" can quickly be made part of a rat's repertoire by arranging for food (reinforcement) to be presented only when that response is made. This must be done in gradual steps and is accomplished by selectively (differentially) reinforcing the rat's successive approximations of a complete roll.

We would begin by first observing that our subject, as he moves about the chamber, sometimes "leans" just a little bit farther to the right than at other times. By paying close attention to these leans, we could withhold reinforcement of all positions except those involving leaning moderately to the right. We would selectively reinforce only that response designated as "a moderate lean to his right." The conditioning paradigm would then look like this:

(1) $R(\text{upright position})---/--\rightarrow S^{R+} (\text{food})$

(2) $R(\text{slight right lean})---/--\rightarrow S^{R+} (\text{food})$

(3) $R(\text{moderate right lean})-----\rightarrow S^{R+} (\text{food})$

By such a procedure, we can extinguish the more "upright" positions and can selectively reinforce moderate leans in the direction of the specified criterion. As a result, the rat more typically will lean to the moderate-right between reinforcements rather than remain completely upright. A second result is that his leans to the right will become more and more excessive. The next step is to increase our "leaning-right" demands, so that we approximate more closely the response we are attempting to establish— that is, a $360°$ roll. Consequently, we would next demand that no responses be reinforced except those that constitute an "extreme lean to the right" (perhaps $150°$). Our paradigm would then take this form:

(4)   R (slight right lean)$— — — / — — → S^{R+}$ (food)

(5)   R (moderate right lean) $— — / — → S^{R+}$ (food)

(6)   R (extreme right lean) $— — — — → S^{R+}$ (food)

As this procedure of successive approximation and differential reinforcement progresses, the rat will finally perform a full roll; thus, an operant that is seldom found in a rat's behavior (except through these special contingencies) will have been conditioned. The only requirements are that each "approximation" is not too large, and that each "new" response in the sequence is *immediately* reinforced when it is emitted. At this point it may appear that we have done little more than offer an exercise in animal training. Nevertheless, when we begin our survey of research studies and case histories in this chapter, the potency of shaping as a technique for modifying maladaptive behavior will be evident.

Schedules of Reinforcement

One of the most important areas of contemporary operant research is concerned with the question of how various schedules of reinforcement affect behavior. A *schedule of reinforcement* refers to the arrangement of reinforcement. It prescribes reinforcement either in terms of some temporal interval or in terms of the subject's emission of a specified number of responses. For instance, if a reinforcing stimulus follows every response, then reinforcement is taking place according to a continuous schedule of reinforcement. Another possibility is that reinforcement may intermittently succeed a response. Here, reinforcement might follow every tenth response, or every response after some specified length of time had elapsed. Further, we could arrange things so that there would be variation either in the number of responses or in the time which must elapse before a response is reinforced. We could further complicate matters by combining or mixing these schedules and the requirements for reinforcement. Obviously, the possible arrangements of schedules of reinforcement are infinite. The importance of the schedules lies in the fact that they produce very significant differences in the behavior upon which they are contingent.

Some schedules result in very rapid extinction when reinforcement is terminated; other schedules lead to very strong resistance to extinction. Under some schedules, the organism becomes very "emotional," and his behavior is quite erratic; under others he appears calm and "unruffled." The point to be made is that, in the laboratory analysis of behavior, the study of reinforcement schedules is of primary interest to researchers; and the potential of these studies in the modification of behavior is great.

A final comment should be made regarding reinforcement. Many individuals are similar with respect to the stimuli that will reinforce their behavior; but the relative efficacy of reinforcing stimuli is subject to large individual differences. With any given patient, a therapist sometimes must "search" for an effective reinforcing stimulus before modification can be started. This search might include a look at the literature involving patients with similar backgrounds and "problems," or it might involve direct empirical tests with various stimuli believed to have reinforcing value for the patient. In any event, one of the initial steps in this kind of modification is the determination of an effective, easily manipulated reinforcer.

With this in mind, we are now ready to review some studies in which positive reinforcement, extinction, shaping, and reinforcement schedules are brought to bear in the modification of maladaptive operant behavior. As we did when we considered the modification of respondent behavior, we should attend to the three basic questions that the behavior technologist holds as a guide: (1) What is the behavior to be modified? (2) What are the stimuli currently maintaining the behavior? (3) What are the variables which will produce the appropriate behavior modification?

Survey of Research and Case Histories

The first study in our review demonstrates the very powerful effect that properly contingent reinforcement has on an individual's behavior. The case involved the conditioning of an 18-year-old male patient, who was described—by the institution where he was inmated—as a "vegetative idiot" (Fuller, 1949). Though he occasionally opened his mouth, blinked, or slightly moved his arms, head, and shoulders, he exhibited no other behavior. In fact, he was unable to eat by himself and had been "spoon-fed" all his life. The institution personnel who had been charged with caring for him felt certain that learning, in any form, was impossible for this patient; and, they asserted, he had not learned anything in his entire life. Nevertheless, in only four sessions the operant conditioning employed by Fuller produced remarkable changes (remembering that we are here concerned with a so-called human "vegetable," who had been deemed "incapable" of learning).

It was decided that an attempt would be made to condition the patient to raise his right arm to a vertical position. The reinforcing stimulus chosen was a warm sugar-milk solution, which was to be administered into the mouth of the patient through a syringe. Prior to the beginning of training, the boy was deprived of food for 15 hours in order to make it likely that the milk would function as a positive reinforcer. During the first session, the milk solution was given to the patient immediately whenever he happened to raise his arm. By the fourth (last) session, arm-raising had become "definite and discrete," occurring at the rate of three responses per minute. The participants in the study were of the opinion that, with time, other operants could be conditioned.

Besides offering the reader a quick glimpse of a reinforcing stimulus in operation, this study also provides interest because of its historical significance. It was one of the earliest attempts to apply the principles derived from the laboratory study of infra-human subjects to practical behavior modification with humans.

A more recent report dealing with the reduction of a conditioned operant, tantrum behavior, was done by Williams (1959). The operation in this case is a rather clear instance of the effective use of the operant extinction procedure. The subject was a 21-month-old boy who had been ill during most of his infancy and, as a result, had been given excessive attention. Unfortunately, though his health was restored, he still demanded the special care and concern that was given during his convalescence. Of particular discomfort to his parents was the boy's insistence that at bedtime they give him unqualified attendance until he fell asleep. This necessitated "dutiful concern" by one of the parents of from one-half hour to two hours at each bedtime. If the parent attempted to leave before the boy fell asleep, the boy began a tantrum and continued to scream and fuss until the parent returned.

It was finally decided that these tantrums should be removed by simply withholding the reinforcement which supported this tyrant-like behavior. The reinforcement, in this case, was identified as the parents "return and consequent attention" whenever the screaming and fussing occurred. Extinction, it was felt, could be accomplished by "not returning" whenever a tantrum was in effect—thereby terminating the response-reinforcement contingency.

Thereafter, as Williams reported, the boy was put "to bed in a leisurely and relaxed fashion. After bedtime pleasantries, the parent left the bedroom and closed the door. S (the boy) screamed and raged, but the parent did not re-enter the room." A record was maintained of the duration of each tantrum, and the data showed that the boy's behavior paralleled that of a typical extinction curve. After tantrums were no longer reinforced, the behavior occurred at a high frequency, gradually diminished, and then terminated altogether. By about the tenth "bedtime" after the extinction procedure was begun, "S no longer whimpered, fussed, or cried when the parent left the room. Rather, he smiled as they left. The parents felt that he made happy sounds until he dropped off to sleep." Sometime later, when an aunt put the boy to bed, some tantrum behavior recurred and she inadvertently reinforced it. Data were then gathered on a second extinction series, and by the ninth session the screaming and fussing again dropped to zero. No additional episodes of tantrum behavior have been reported in the two years since the second extinction series was begun. As Williams concluded:

> It should be emphasized that the treatment in this case did not involve aversive punishment. All that was done was to remove the reinforcement. Extinction of the tyrant-like behavior then occurred.

> No unfortunate side or after-effects of this treatment were observed. At three and three-quarters years of age, S appeared to be a friendly, expressive, outgoing child (1959).

Positive reinforcement is of primary importance in the effective modification of maladaptive operant behavior, but there are many situations in which an effective reinforcer is not apparent. One way of finding a stimulus or an event that is likely to have reinforcing efficacy is indicated by the Premack principle (1959). Briefly stated, the Premack principle asserts that if some specific behavior is more probable than another, then that behavior may be used to strengthen a less probable behavior. To strengthen a less probable behavior, one has only to make the presentation of the highly probable behavior contingent upon the occurrence of the less probable. For instance, if young Robert thoroughly enjoys an outing with his uncle but detests raking the lawn, one could condition "lawn raking" by making an "outing with uncle" contingent upon a well-groomed lawn. In this arrangement, an "outing" would operate as a reinforcing stimulus for "lawn raking."

The Premack principle was applied effectively in the following case, reported by a group of behavior technologists who altered the mildly maladaptive responses of three nursery school children (Homme, deBaca, Deirue, Steinhorst, & Rickert, 1963). Whenever these 3-year-old youngsters were asked to be seated, they often failed to heed the request, continuing instead to run about the room, scream, push chairs, and attend to other distractions. Homme and his colleagues decided that these non-sitting, noisy behaviors might constitute Premack's description of "highly probable" behavior. If so, the experimenters reasoned, why not use these highly probable events to reinforce the less probable response of "sitting quietly in a chair"? With this in view, the experimenters made the high probability behavior contingent upon more appropriate nursery school behavior, such as sitting quietly or looking at the blackboard. The children were told to sit down and attend to the nursery schedule. Intermittently this behavior was interrupted by a bell, whereupon the children were told to "run and scream." As the authors wrote:

> The Ss would then leap to their feet and run around the room screaming. At another signal they would stop. At this time they would get another signal and an instruction to engage in some other behavior which, on a quasi-random schedule, might be one of high or low probability. At a later stage, Ss earned tokens for low probability behavior which could later be used to "buy" the opportunity for higher probability activities.
>
> With this kind of procedure, control was virtually perfect after a few days. For example, when Ss were requested to "sit and look at the blackboard" (an activity which in the past had intermittently been interrupted by the signal for some higher probability behavior), they were under such good control that an observer, new on the scene, almost certainly would have assumed extensive aversive control was being used (1963).

The final part of the quote should be stressed. No punishments (aversive stimuli) were brought to bear in manipulating the environment to produce the adaptive nursery school behavior; as a consequence, none of the negative side effects of punishment were in evidence. In fact, the atmosphere of harmony that existed in the situation is one of the more outstanding features of control maintained by positive reinforcement.

A more extreme instance of maladaptive behavior was reported by Isaacs, Thomas, and Goldiamond (1960), who reinstated verbal behavior in psychotics. The particular case we will consider involved a 40-year-old patient who had been diagnosed as a catatonic schizophrenic. He had become completely mute upon commitment and had remained mute for *19 years*. This study clearly demonstrates the function not only of positive reinforcement but also of *shaping* in the modification of behavior. Further, it touches on two points that are relevant to this chapter: (1) the difficulty often encountered in finding a reinforcing stimulus; and (2) the rapid progress which may ensue when one is located. The case of Patient A, as given by the authors, is presented below in its entirety.

Patient A

The *S* was brought to a group therapy session with other chronic schizophrenics (who were verbal), but he sat in the position in which he was placed and continued the withdrawal behaviors which characterized him. He remained impassive and stared ahead even when cigarettes, which other members accepted, were offered to him and were waved before his face. At one session, when *E* removed cigarettes from his pocket, a package of chewing gum accidentally fell out. The *S*'s eyes moved toward the gum and then returned to their usual position. This response was chosen by *E* as one with which he would start to work, using the method of successive approximation. (This method finds use where *E* desires to produce responses which are not present in the current repertoire of the organism and which are considerably removed from those which are available. The *E* then attempts to 'shape' the available behaviors into the desired form, capitalizing upon both the variability and regularity of successive behaviors. The shaping process involves the reinforcement of those parts of a selected response which are successively in the desired direction and the nonreinforcement of those which are not. For example, a pigeon may be initially reinforced when it moves its head. When this movement occurs regularly, only an upward movement may be reinforced with downward movement not reinforced. The pigeon may now stretch its neck, with this movement reinforced. Eventually, the pigeon may be trained to peck at a disc which was initially high above its head and at which it would normally never peck. In the case of the psychotic under discussion, the succession was eye movement, which brought into play occasional facial movements, including those of the mouth, lip movements, vocalizations, words utterance, and finally, verbal behavior.)

The *S* met individually with *E* three times a week. Group sessions also continued. The following sequence of procedures was introduced in the private sessions. Although the weeks are numbered consecutively, they did not follow at regular intervals since other duties kept *E* from seeing *S* every week.

Weeks 1, 2. A stick of gum was held before *S*'s face, and *E* waited until *S*'s eyes moved toward it. When this response occurred, *E* as a consequence gave him the gum. By the end of the second week response probability in the presence of the gum was increased to such an extent that *S*'s eyes moved toward the gum as soon as it was held up.

Weeks 3, 4. The *E* now held the gum before *S*, waiting until he noticed movement in *S*'s lips before giving it to him. Toward the end of the first session of the third week, a lip movement spontaneously occurred, which *E* promptly reinforced. By the end of this week, both lip movement and eye movement occurred when the gum was held up. The *E* then withheld giving *S* the gum until *S* spontaneously made a vocalization at which time *E* gave *S* the gum. By the end of this week, holding up the gum readily occasioned eye movement toward it, lip movement, and a vocalization resembling a croak.

Weeks 5, 6. The E held up the gum, and said, "Say gum, gum," repeating these words each time S vocalized. Giving S the gum was made contingent upon vocalizations increasingly approximating "gum." At the sixth session (at the end of Week 6), when E said, "Say gum, gum," S suddenly said: "Gum please." This response was accompanied by reinstatement of other responses of this class, that is, S answered questions regarding his name and age.

Thereafter, he responded to questions by E both in individual sessions and in group sessions, but answered no one else. Response to the discriminative stimuli of the room generalized to E on the ward; he greeted E on two occasions in the group room. He read from signs in E's office upon request by E.

Since the response now seemed to be under the strong stimulus control of E, the person, attempt was made to generalize the stimulus to other people. Accordingly, a nurse was brought into the private room; S smiled at her. After a month, he began answering her questions. Later, when he brought his coat to a volunteer worker on the ward, she interpreted the gesture as a desire to go outdoors and conducted him there. Upon informing E of the incident, she was instructed to obey S only as a consequence of explicit verbal requests by him. The S thereafter vocalized requests. These instructions have now been given to other hospital personnel, and S regularly initiates verbal requests when non-verbal requests have no reinforcing consequences. Upon being taken to the commissary, he said "Ping pong," to the volunteer worker and played a game with her. Other patients, visitors, and members of hospital-society-at-large continue, however, to interpret nonverbal requests and to reinforce them by obeying S (1960).

Considering the length of time that this patient had been mute, the accomplishments made by the experimenters were resounding. It should be noted, however, that although verbal behavior was reinstated, progress might have been even more impressive, and the "cure" more complete, if other persons in the patient's environment had ceased to reinforce his non-verbal requests. At present, environments geared to more pervasive control than that which prevailed in the present study are becoming widespread. These environments are established in the wards of many "mental" hospitals and are called *token economies*. A token economy is arranged by training and instructing *all* the personnel on a given ward regarding contingencies of reinforcement so that they are consistent in reinforcing the adaptive behaviors of a given patient and extinguishing the maladaptive. It may be surmised that in such a milieu the remarkable achievements made by the patient would have been extended and expanded considerably.

In a case reported by Sulzer (1965), social reinforcement was used in the modification of the maladaptive behavior of a patient who came to the psychologist because of problems with alcohol. More traditional approaches to a solution of his problem had failed. He had a long history of intoxication that frequently precipitated aversive consequences; and even though he often pledged that he would stop drinking, he was unable to do so. In this case, solitary drinking was not part of the problem; it was found that most of his imbibing was done in a few specific social and vocational situations. His job required that he frequent taverns and similar establishments, and he was also likely to overindulge himself with alcohol when he was with friends. As the interview progressed, the patient mentioned that he was presently about to lose the friendship of two life-long companions who had begun to find his drunkenness objectionable.

With this bit of information, Sulzer enlisted the help of these two men to "create a situation in which social reinforcement for non-alcoholic drinking might be developed." The contingencies of reinforcement were simple. After work the patient would meet with his two friends for the usual social chat. In contrast to the past, however, the patient was permitted to drink only soft beverages. Moreover, the two friends were instructed to leave their friend immediately if he ordered any alcoholic beverage.

The cooperation of the patient's friends was also enlisted for other drinking situations. For example, if there was to be any occasion on which the patient would serve alcoholic drinks at a party, his friends were also to be invited. Again, they were told to remain only so long as the patient did not drink. With this simple arrangement of social reinforcement contingent upon "non-drinking," the decrease in his drinking was remarkably rapid. There was only one minor instance of "regression" to alcohol, but it was brief and transitory. The patient had become a teetotaler.

Though the major reinforcement in this case was the social attention of the patient's friends, there were a number of additional factors which probably expedited the more adaptive response of non-drinking. Bartenders he met in the course of his business, as well as other people, began to respond with more friendliness as his alcohol-related obnoxiousness was no longer extant; and this increase in friendliness probably functioned as a strong positive reinforcer. Additionally, his therapist also expressed verbal and facial approval of non-drinking behavior, which very likely provided "extra" reinforcement. In any event, as far as is known, the patient has maintained his sobriety.

This case in no way is intended to imply that the social reinforcement technique used with this patient would be very effective with the average "alcoholic." It is not very probable that social attention would operate as the most important positive reinforcer for the typical person who drinks in excess. However, the case does again point up the radical changes which can be effected on operant behavior when, fortuitously or otherwise, a strong reinforcer is found that pertains to a given individual. When such a reinforcer is discovered and made properly contingent on the behavior to be modified, the psychologist employing this operant conditioning technique is well on his way to a successful resolution of the patient's maladaptiveness.

In rounding out our sampling of the literature, we have still to consider the use of schedules of reinforcement in the modification of particular cases of maladaptive operant behavior. The study of reinforcement schedules holds great promise for therapy, but very little research which is relevant to this primer has as yet appeared in the journals. The study which probably is most closely attuned to the purpose of this book was conducted by Haughton and Ayllon (1966). Their study was concerned with the demonstration of certain environmental events which control operant behavior, and with the question of how these events can account for the development and elimination of operant responding. Haughton and Ayllon elected to use a repetitive, "purposeless" response in the demonstration, because, traditionally, such responses are difficult to treat and are accounted for within the framework of psychoanalytic or psychodynamic theories. These investigators, in contrast to traditional views, considered these repetitive response patterns, as well as related "abnormal behavior patterns," to be within the pale of behavioral analysis and thus subject to change through behavior modification techniques.

The subject was a 54-year-old woman who had been hospitalized for 23 years. She was generally quite idle and did little on the ward except smoke. The researchers decided to condition a novel response (one which could be classified as repetitive and "purposeless") for their demonstration, using cigarettes as reinforcers. The response they selected was "holding the broom in an upright position."

After the patient had been deprived of cigarettes for a period of time, she was approached by a staff member and handed a broom. Whenever she held the broom in a manner approximating the position specified by the experimenters, she was again approached and given a cigarette. Her broom holding was gradually shaped through cigarette reinforcement until the proper position was finally assumed. When this behavior was conditioned, the reinforcement for "holding the broom while in an upright position" was put on an intermittent, variable-interval (VI) schedule. This means that the patient was given reinforcement only after a certain amount of time had elapsed, and then only if she was emitting the broom-holding response. This schedule, rather than one of continuous reinforcement, was put into effect for two major reasons: first, a VI schedule produces and supports very persistent, relatively unvariable behavior; second, it permits economy of the reinforcer and assures its continued effectiveness. Had the patient been given a cigarette on every minute she was broom-holding, it is likely that the cigarette-reinforcement-effect would have been reduced. With these contingencies in control, the patient was soon conditioned to the position, which she maintained for long durations. Then, at a later date, an extinction procedure was begun (broom-holding was no longer reinforced), and the response was eliminated. In a follow-up study two years later, there was no record of a recurrence of the response.

That the repetitive broom-holding response paralleled many everyday behavioral responses leading to hospitalization is suggested in the statements made by two psychiatrists who were asked to observe and evaluate the patient. The psychiatrists' evaluations, given below, help place the patient's behavior in clinical perspective:

> Dr. A's evaluation of the patient's behavior was:
>
> The broom represents to this patient some essential perceptual element in her field of consciousness. How it should have become so is uncertain; on Freudian grounds it could be interpreted symbolically, on behavioral grounds it could perhaps be interpreted as a habit which has become essential to her peace of mind. Whatever may be the case, it is certainly a stereotyped form of behavior such as is commonly seen in rather regressed schizophrenics and is rather analogous to the way small children or infants refuse to be parted from some favorite toy, piece of rag, etc.
>
> Dr. B's evaluation of the patient's behavior was:
>
> Her constant and compulsive pacing holding a broom in the manner she does could be seen as a ritualistic procedure, a magical action. When regression conquers the associative process, primitive and archaic forms of thinking control the behavior. Symbolism is a predominant mode of expression of deep seated unfulfilled desires and instinctual impulses. By magic, she controls others, cosmic powers are at her disposal and inanimate objects become living creatures.
>
> Her broom could be then:
>
> 1. a child that gives her love and she gives him in return her devotion;
> 2. a phallic symbol;
> 3. the sceptre of an omnipotent queen.
>
> Her rhythmic and prearranged pacing in a certain space are not similar to the compulsions of a neurotic, but because this is a far more irrational, far more controlled behavior from a primitive thinking, this is a magical procedure in which the patient carries out her wishes, expressed in a way that is far beyond our solid, rational and conventional way of thinking and acting (Haughton & Ayllon, 1966, pp. 97-98).

The above are classic examples of clinical interpretations. But why, in fact, was the patient really holding the broom? The behavior therapist would say, quite simply, that she held the broom because she had been operantly conditioned on a variable-interval schedule of reinforcement for doing so!

Haughton and Ayllon concluded their study by noting that "the apparent uselessness and irrelevance of the patient's behavior is indeed the hallmark of behavior often clinically described as 'compulsive' or 'psychotic.' Yet examination of some of the environmental conditions under which the response was developed, may make it easier to understand how similar classes of behavior are developed and maintained by environmental contingencies (1966, p. 98)."

This completes our sampling of the literature dealing with the application of positive reinforcement in the modification of maladaptive behavior. The selections were well chosen if the reader now has an appreciation of the importance of positive reinforcement, shaping, and schedules in the practical control and modification of behavior.

Selected Readings

Reports on the outcome of *token economies* have been very encouraging, and the use of this form of therapy is spreading quite rapidly. A description of how the token system was developed, along with a report of a series of experiments evaluating its effectiveness, is found in:

> Ayllon, T. & Azrin, N. H. *The token economy: A motivational system for therapy and rehabilitation.* New York: Appleton-Century-Crofts, 1968.

For the reader who would like an elaboration of operant conditioning principles as they might be applied in a "utopian" society, this widely acclaimed novel is strongly recommended. The society in the book is structured and maintained primarily on the basis of contingencies of positive reinforcement.

> Skinner, B. F. *Walden two.* New York: Macmillan, 1948.

A thorough coverage of the nature of reinforcement theory is provided in a short, but very adequate, new paperback book by Fred S. Keller, who is one of the pioneers of behavior modification.

> Keller, F. S. *Learning: Reinforcement theory.* (2nd. ed.) New York: Random House, 1969.

5

The Aversive Stimulus and Operant Behavior

Aversivity, Escape, and Avoidance

The variable that concerns us in this chapter is the *aversive stimulus*, which may be defined as any stimulus which an organism (if given the opportunity) will escape from, avoid, or terminate. An aversive stimulus is one which the layman would generally speak of as causing pain or discomfort. We have simply given the layman's term a little more precision by operationally defining it with reference to what the organism does in the presence of such a stimulus.

If an organism does something that actually removes or terminates an aversive stimulus such as electric shock, then the organism is said to be engaging in *escape behavior.* If the organism does something to postpone or prevent pending aversivity, then he is said to be engaging in *avoidance behavior.* Both types of behavior are supported or conditioned through *negative reinforcement.* Any response that is immediately followed by the termination of an aversive stimulus will become conditioned. That is, a response which terminates aversivity will increase in frequency or strength. When behavior is thus strengthened, the operation involved is called negative reinforcement.

The stimulus used in negative reinforcement might be one which is "naturally" aversive to the organism, such as electric shock, or the stimulus might be one which has become aversive through respondent conditioning. For instance, it will be recalled from Chapter 2 that a tone which is repeatedly paired with shock will itself come to elicit some of the aversive responses (for example, fear) associated with shock. In any event, whether a "natural" or a conditioned aversive stimulus is employed, a response which terminates or avoids it will increase in strength through negative reinforcement.

The paradigm for negative reinforcement is quite similar to that of positive reinforcement, the only difference being a slight change in notation to indicate that an aversive (negative) stimulus is the reinforcer, and that the reinforcement operation involves the removal of a stimulus rather than its presentation following the response. Let us illustrate the process. If a rat is placed in an experimental chamber in which the grid floor is electrified, and if the animal's bar-pressing terminates the shock for ten seconds, he will quickly be conditioned to the bar-press response. The paradigm may be diagrammed as follows:

$$R \text{ (bar press)} - - - - \rightarrow S^{R-} \text{ (shock termination)}$$

There are numerous everyday responses that are maintained by negative reinforcement: cupping the ears when there is a series of loud noises; turning the thermostat down when the room has become too warm and stuffy; and saying "Get off my foot" when someone has inadvertently covered your shoe with his. There are many other responses reinforced in the same way; but one should remember that reinforcement, whether positive or negative, always refers to an operation which increases the strength of some behavior upon which the reinforcement is contingent. Now let us take a look at the reverse of any reinforcement operation: punishment.

Punishment

The operation of punishment is constituted by either of two events. The first of these occurs when an organism receives an aversive stimulus (a negative reinforcer) as the consequence of a response. For example, returning once again to our rat in his experimental chamber, let us imagine that he is pressing the bar for food as usual. For this exercise, however, suppose we change the conditions just slightly so that, as a consequence of each bar-press, the rat also receives five seconds of moderate shock. This is the first instance of punishment.

A second form of punishment occurs when a positive reinforcer is withdrawn or withheld as a consequence of an organism's response. Suppose, again, that the rat is on a continuous schedule of positive reinforcement, that each bar-press is succeeded by a food pellet. Now let's add a blue light to his environment, arranging conditions in such a way that, periodically, the light comes on for ten seconds. We might further arrange that, whenever the blue light is on, a bar-press by the rat alters the reinforcement schedule so that all reinforcement is withheld for fifteen minutes. In this case, the rat's response in the presence of the blue light terminates the prevailing response-reinforcement contingency, and the second form of response-contingent punishment has been put into effect.

In both of these instances, the most predominant result is the suppression of the response that produced punishment. This suppression offers the behavior technologist the opportunity to then condition other responses which are viewed as potentially more "desirable" additions to the organism's repertoire. Often these more desirable responses are incompatible with the punished response, thereby increasing the probability that they—rather than the punished response—will be emitted on future occasions.

Besides the suppression of behavior, punishment has a number of other effects on the organism. There are autonomic effects, depending upon the schedule and intensity (among other things) of the aversive stimulus. But more important for our discussion is the fact that, if used injudiciously, aversive controls may promote maladaptive behavior rather than increase adaptive responses. Used sparingly, and under the proper contingencies, the aversive stimulus is a very effective variable in behavior modification; nevertheless, it can be harmful to the health and welfare of the organism if it is not used wisely.

This chapter has presented a general overview of the aversive stimulus and operant behavior—an overview that includes four distinct operations, which may be summarized as follows:

1. If a *positive reinforcer* is *presented* to an organism following a response, the result is *positive reinforcement*.

2. If a *positive reinforcer* is *withdrawn* following an organism's response, the result is *punishment*.

3. If a *negative reinforcer* is *presented* to an organism following a response, the result is *punishment*.

4. If a *negative reinforcer* is *withdrawn* following an organism's response, the result is *negative reinforcement*.

With these operations in mind, let us now consider several studies and cases in which the aversive stimulus was applied to the modification of maladaptive behavior.

Survey of Research and Case Histories

One sub-section of a study by Ayllon and Michael (1959) neatly illustrates the manner in which weak, or infrequent, behavior may be strengthened by escape and avoidance conditioning (negative reinforcement). It also introduces an additional point of considerable general interest: Once behavior has been conditioned, the contingencies which were operative in its establishment need not remain in effect for the behavior to be maintained. For instance, though negative reinforcement might be necessary to bring about some "socially desirable" response, the new response itself may thereafter promote positive consequences (reinforcement) which will support its continuance. This kind of reinforcement "changeover" is evident in the following report.

Janet and Mary, two hospitalized patients who generally refused to eat unless helped by nurses, were the subjects of the investigation. Caring for these women was quite time-consuming for the hospital personnel, since both patients insisted upon being spoon-fed at mealtime and would not eat otherwise. About the only thing that either of the patients "cared about" was the neat and clean appearance of her clothing. In recognition of the patients' one identifiable concern in life, the therapists decided that "accidental" food-spilling (on the patients' clothing during spoon-feeding) would be used as an aversive stimulus. Either patient could escape the "soiling," of course, by taking the spoon and feeding herself after food-spilling had begun. Alternatively, she could completely avoid soiling by feeding herself at the beginning of the meal.

The authors believed that this negative reinforcement procedure would strengthen self-feeding. They also felt that after self-feeding had been well established in this manner, other environmental variables (convenience, social stimulation, and so forth) would come into play and function as positive reinforcers—thereby maintaining self-feeding in the absence of any aversivity. The program led to encouraging changes in the behavior of both patients, and, at the time the report was written, self-feeding had been sustained for over ten months.

The subtleties involved in the administration of this program may be appreciated by considering the instructions that were given to the hospital personnel. The nurses were instructed as follows:

> Continue spoonfeeding the patient; but from now on, do so in such a careless way that the patient will have a few drops of food fall on her dress. Be sure not to overdo the food dropping, since what we want to convey to the patient is that it is difficult to spoonfeed a grown-up person, and not that we are mean to her. What we expect

is that the patient will find it difficult to depend on your skill to feed her. You will still be feeding her, but you will simply be less efficient in doing a good job of it. As the patient likes having her clothes clean, she will have to choose between feeding herself and keeping her clothes clean, or being fed by others and risking getting her clothes soiled. Whenever she eats on her own, be sure to stay with her for awhile (3 minutes is enough) talking to her, or simply being seated with her. We do this to reinforce her eating on her own. In the experience of the patient, people become nicer when she eats on her own (Ayllon & Michael, 1959).

In Mary's case, this procedure produced a rather "happy ending." As Ayllon and Michael reported:

Since the patient's hospital admission had been based on her refusal to eat, accompanied by statements that the food was poisoned, the success of the program led to her discharge. It is to be noted that although nothing was done to deal directly with her claims that the food was poisoned, these statements dropped out of her repertoire as she began to eat on her own (1959).

In considering the role of punishment in operant control, we turn first to a study by Wilde (1964) which clearly incorporates one form of punishment that we discussed earlier: the presentation of an aversive stimulus as a consequence of a response. The subjects in this case were "addicted" cigarette smokers who were alarmed about the "habit" and who wanted to give it up. The apparatus and procedure used in the experiment were described by Wilde as follows:

The subject under treatment sits at a table opposite the experimenter. On the table is a horizontal turning disk of 60 cm diameter, on which two electric ventilator heaters have been placed at an angle of 40 degrees. On one of the ventilators a cylinder has been mounted so as to direct the outcoming air (of about 45 degrees centigrade) into the face of the subject. At the back of this ventilator heater, where the air from the room is sucked in, a perforated metal soap-dish has been mounted, into which a number (e.g. 10) of lit cigarettes have been placed. These cigarettes are smoked by the ventilator and their smoke comes out diffused in hot air. This mixture of smoke and hot air is used as the unconditioned aversive stimulus. It is tolerated for some 10-15 sec. and is experienced by the subject as a combination of the disagreeable attributes of cigarettes (an "essence of cigarette").

The second ventilator (without cylinder) produces a somewhat slower stream of air of room temperature (without heat or smoke) in which a little bit of menthol from an aerosol is diffused on an unpredictable schedule in 50 per cent of the trials. This second stimulus (the "reward") is experienced as being very agreeable and refreshing, as a "true relief." When the reward stimulus is presented, the subject is also permitted to take a small peppermint from a small dish whenever he likes (substitute behavior to be learnt). The sweet is usually consumed within 10 seconds.

During the treatment sessions, the smoker is invited to light a cigarette of his preferred brand. Simultaneously, the aversive stimulus is administered. The smoker has to keep the cigarette in his mouth until he cannot tolerate the aversive stimulus in combination with his own cigarette any longer. As soon as the smoker puts his cigarette out and pronounces the autosuggestive phrase "I want to give up smoking" (or something similar), the rewarding stimulus is administered and he is allowed to take a peppermint if he wishes. The administration of the two stimuli is carried out easily by rotating the turntable. The cigarette put out by the subject is added to the ones smoked by the heated ventilator. The trials are repeated a number of times depending on the subject's report of his tolerance (6-20 times). Then the aversive stimulus is cut out and the smoker is invited to light a cigarette without the aversive stimulus. This is done in order to have him feel that the cigarette itself has become offensive and sickening. This cigarette is usually put out as quickly as the ones during aversive stimulation, that is after 2-3 draws. The session is then ended with some instructions to the smoker under treatment which have to be followed until the next session 24 hours later ("if you happen to feel like a cigarette, try to remember the treatment session, try to experience the sensation of relief when putting out the cigarette and saying that you want to give up smoking, take a peppermint or something similar instead. If you give in nevertheless, keep the cigarette in your mouth until you cannot stand it anymore, and extinguish it"). The treatment is discontinued when the smoker reports that he has not smoked anymore without having to exercise excessive self-control (1964).

At the time of Wilde's article, he had treated seven people with this punishment technique. Of these seven volunteers, three discontinued smoking entirely (after only two 25-minute sessions), one patient changed to a pipe, and one reduced his frequency of smoking to two cigarettes a day. The remaining two subjects stopped their treatment.

Even though the procedure did not lead to completely successful results, the limited success it did enjoy is encouraging. The duration of treatment was very brief; moreover, if the procedure were combined with other techniques, it might become even more efficient. In any event, if further research were to demonstrate that half of those who volunteer for the program may be "cured" of smoking, then that rate in itself would seem to justify this form of aversive control.

Before we conclude our consideration of the Wilde investigation, a cautionary comment is in order. While a response-contingent presentation of an aversive stimulus was clearly in evidence in this study, one cannot deduce that the reduction in smoking is directly attributable to the aversive stimulus alone. Other factors may have been involved. For instance, negative reinforcement may have conditioned the behavior of non-smoking. After all, to "stop smoking" and thereby to avoid any additional treatment (which was very aversive) would constitute a rather strong reinforcer. The reinforcement of the autosuggestions could also have accounted for the results. There are, of course, other factors that may have been at play. In any event, we have seen one instance in which the presentation of an aversive stimulus has been employed as a variable in operant modification. Further research in this area will sharpen and delineate its efficacy.

The first experiment in a project conducted by Ayllon (1963) clearly demonstrates the impact on behavior of the second form of punishment: the withdrawal of a positive reinforcer. In this case, a 47-year-old chronic schizophrenic patient had been giving the nursing staff considerable alarm because of her excessive weight (250 pounds). The woman's weight was considered detrimental to her health, and the nurses had spent much time trying to persuade, coax, and coerce the patient to stop stealing food, as well as to consume more moderate portions of her own rations. Records that had been maintained for nearly a month prior to the experiment indicated that the patient engaged in stealing from other patients during two-thirds of every meal period. The new program was intended to stop this behavior.

To accomplish this, the therapist first assigned the patient to a table in the dining hall, where no one was permitted to sit with her. The nurses were instructed to remove the patient from the dining hall if she either approached someone else's table or picked up unauthorized food. When she engaged in either of these behaviors, she had to forego the meal. In technical terms, the response (stealing food) led to the withdrawal of a positive reinforcer (food).

As a consequence of this punishment operation, the patient's food-stealing response was eliminated in two weeks, whereupon she ate only her normally allotted portion. Upon termination of this treatment, which apparently continued for about a year, the patient's weight had stabilized at 180 pounds, and her physical condition was considered to be excellent.

Ayllon's concluding comments bear very directly on the contrast between the behavior modification orientation, on one side, and the more traditional therapies and the general psychiatric view, on the other. As Ayllon wrote:

> A frequent problem encountered in mental hospitals is overeating. In general this problem is solved by prescribing a reduction diet.

Many patients however, refuse to take a reduction diet and continue overeating. When confronted with this behavior, psychiatric workers generally resort to two types of explanations.

One explanation of overeating points out that only with the active and sincere co-operation of the patient can weight reduction be accomplished. When the patient refuses to co-operate he is regarded as showing more signs of mental illness and all hopes of eliminating overeating come to an end.

Another explanation holds that overeating is not the behavior to be concerned with. Instead, attention is focused on the psychological "needs" of the patient. These "needs" are said to be the causes of the observable behavior, overeating. Therefore the emphasis is on the removal of the cause and not on the symptom or behavior itself. Whatever theoretical merit these explanations may have, it is unfortunate that they fail to suggest practical ways of treating the behavior itself. As a consequence, the patient continues to overeat, often to the detriment of his health.

The current psychiatric emphasis on the resolution of the mental conflict that is presumably at the basis of the symptoms, is perhaps misplaced. What seems to have been forgotten is that behavior problems such as those reported here, prevent the patient from being considered for discharge not only by the hospital personnel but also by the patient's relatives. Indeed, as far as the patient's relatives are concerned, the index of improvement or deterioration is the readily observable behavior and not a detailed account of the mechanics of the mental apparatus.

Many individuals are admitted to mental hospitals because of one or more specific behavior difficulties and not always because of a generalized "mental" disturbance. For example, an individual may go into a mental hospital because he has refused to eat for several days, or because he talks to himself incessantly. If the goal of therapy were behavioral rehabilitation, these problems would be treated and normal eating and normal talking reinstated. However, the current emphasis in psychotherapy is on "mental-conflict resolution" and little or no attention is given to dealing directly with the behavioral problems which prevent the patient from returning to the community (1963).

Fortunately, we feel, the emphasis on "mental-conflict resolution" has decreased, and an ever larger number of psychologists and related professional personnel have become oriented to the behavioral model of "mental illness." The decline of the "medical" model in favor of behavior modification approaches will be discussed at a little greater length in Chapter 7. On this theme, we conclude the present chapter and turn to the two remaining variables which control operant responding: *drive* and the *discriminative stimulus.*

Selected Readings

While there is no text devoted entirely to the effects of the aversive stimulus on behavior, there are a number of books which do provide chapters on this subject. The role of the aversive stimulus in the control of behavior, as presently understood, is given excellent coverage in the following references. For convenience, the appropriate chapters are also listed.

Lundin, R. W. *Personality: A behavioral analysis.* New York: Macmillan, 1969. See Chapters IX-XII.

Reynolds, G. S. *A primer of operant conditioning.* Glenview, Ill.: Scott, Foresman, 1968. See Chapter IX.

Research and case histories on the application of aversive control typically appear in nearly every issue of the following journals, and the reader can quickly increase his familiarity with this field by looking through a few recent issues.

Behaviour Research and Therapy

Journal of Applied Behavior Analysis

6

Other Variables
in Operant Control

Deprivation—Satiation

One of the two remaining variables in operant control is *drive*, or the deprivation-satiation dimension. It is regarded as a basic variable because, with other contingencies held constant, a variation in drive will further affect the strength or probability of an organism's behavior.

In order to illustrate the operation of drive, suppose that we arrange once again—through response-contingent food reinforcement—for a rat to press a bar. Let us also suppose that our subject has been deprived of food for 48 hours before our experiment. While he is in the experimental chamber, we would observe that he presses the bar at a fairly high and steady rate. In manipulating drive in this example, we might simply remove the animal from the chamber and permit him to free-feed for one hour in his home cage. Free-feeding for one hour should satiate the rat; and if satiation has in fact occurred, we have drastically altered the animal's prevailing drive condition.

The effect of this operation could easily be ascertained by returning the rat to the experimental chamber. Even with the bar-press reinforcement contingency still in effect, we would then note that the strength of this operant had greatly diminished. It is very likely, in fact, that bar-pressing would not have occurred at all. Obviously, this is a very simple operation. We increase or decrease drive by depriving the organism of the appropriate stimulus, or by satiating the subject with the reinforcing stimulus. Drive is then reflected in the rate of bar-press responding, or in the strength of the relevant operant.

There are many everyday examples of the use of this variable. For instance, a host who holds a very late evening dinner may do so in order to increase the "enthusiasm" with which his guests approach and undertake the meal. A restaurateur, on the other hand, wishing to offer smaller portions of the main course without complaint from his patrons, might provide many tasty, but inexpensive, hors d'oeuvres. In general, however, even though the drive operation is quite simple, most people do not employ it either very deliberately or with a full appreciation of its many applications. In fact, with respect to the efficient and systematic manipulation of this variable in the control of maladaptive behavior, its use has come to the fore only recently with the growth of the behavior modification movement. Before studying this literature, we will pause to elaborate on the final major variable in operant control.

The Discriminative Stimulus

A *discriminative stimulus* is formally defined as a stimulus that sets the occasion for reinforced responding. With reinforcement and drive constant, the probability of the occurrence of an operant can be made functionally dependent upon the presence or absence of a discriminative stimulus. Let us clarify the notion of stimulus control by looking again at our rat in his experimental chamber. As he is pressing the bar for food, suppose that we modify the contingencies slightly by attaching a light to the inside of the chamber. Whenever the light is on and the subject presses the bar, he will—as before—receive the food reinforcement; however, when the light is off, bar-presses will not be succeeded by a food pellet. As the light-on, light-off sequence is continued, bar-presses in the presence of the light will increase, and presses in the absence of light will decrease. Eventually, when the light is turned on, the rat will respond by immediately pressing the bar. Outside of the light-on condition he will not engage the bar at all. The light has thus become a discriminative stimulus, and the bar-press is under stimulus control. This three-term paradigm, which represents most well-established operant behavior, is given below:

$$S^D \text{ (light on)} - - - \rightarrow R \text{ (bar-pressing)} - - - \rightarrow S^{R+} \text{ (food)}$$

The discriminative stimulus (S^D), as a result of the discrimination training we described, is now in control of the response. As mentioned, this three-term paradigm is characteristic of most operant behavior. While original conditioning may take place in a "free" operant situation, as illustrated in the first operant paradigm of Chapter 4 ($R - - \rightarrow S^{R+}$), this nearly always changes. Sooner or later some stimulus will gain control of the response, either by accident or by a special environmental arrangement, because responses in the presence of that stimulus are differentially reinforced. For example, when a child first emits the word "Da-da," the happy and surprised parents or relatives will do any number of things to reinforce the response just to keep it in the child's behavioral repertoire. However, as time goes on, the adults become more and more likely to reinforce the response differentially and to offer the child their attention and praise only when the word is uttered specifically in response to the father.

Before we turn to the literature, one final comment is in order. Stimulus generalization (and the related process, generalization of extinction) is a phenomenon that is characteristic of the S^D, just as it is characteristic of a respondent CS; that is, stimuli that are similar to the original S^D will also gain some control over the response. In our paradigm, once discrimination has been established to the light, other lights of different brightness (or color) will also have some control over bar-pressing. Similarly, in the case of the child who has just learned the word "Da-da," we would frequently find him saying "Da-da" in response to the presence of men other than his father. This completes our introduction to drive and stimulus control, and we can now turn to some of the research and cases in which they have been applied.

Survey of Research and Case Histories

A very clear instance of the satiation technique as used in the control of behavior was offered in one portion of a study by Ayllon (1963). The patient was a 47-year-old woman, diagnosed as a "chronic schizophrenic," who engaged in a number of behaviors which were somewhat disrupting to the nursing staff. One of these behaviors was the hoarding in her own room of the towels belonging to the hospital ward. During her tenure in the hospital, the patient had been accumulating towels; in fact, she kept about 20 in her room at any given time, even though the nurses tried to recover them. When towels were retrieved by the nurses, the patient simply replenished her supply. Since the patient's hoarding put an extra burden on the nurses, it was decided that some new attempt should be made to change this behavior. All other attempts had failed. Within this context, a stimulus satiation program was undertaken.

At the beginning of the program, no more towels were removed from the patient's room; on the contrary, periodically throughout the day a nurse would take the patient a towel and offer it without comment. Each day the number of towels given to the patient was increased, until, by the third week, she was receiving approximately 60 towels daily. When the total number of hoarded towels reached 625, she began to remove them from her room. This continued until the towels "on hand" reached a reasonable number. Over the next year, the average number of towels kept in her room each week (1.5) assumed more "civilized" proportions.

In analyzing the "dynamics" of the patient's marked change in behavior toward towels, the author suggested that, initially, towels functioned as reinforcing stimuli. But as the number of towels drastically increased, they began to lose their value as reinforcers and, rather, became aversive. This aversivity led the patient to remove them, thereby terminating the aversive consequences. That this analysis may be correct is suggested in the patient's comments as the program proceeded. For instance, when handed another towel in the earlier stages she replied: "Oh, you found it for me, thank you." As aversivity began to build, her comments became a bit more negative: "Don't give me no more towels. I've got enough." Or: "Take them towels away . . . I can't sit here all night and fold towels." Finally, toward the end of the satiation program, she responded to the nurses with the comments "Get these dirty towels out of here," and "I can't drag anymore of these towels, I just can't do it." From the patient's exclamations, it would appear that the towels had indeed become aversive and that the author's analysis contains some merit.

Ayllon's own comments offer additional perspective on the value of therapy from the behavior technologist's viewpoint:

> The ward nurses who had undergone a three year training in psychiatric nursing, found it difficult to reconcile the procedure in this experiment with their psychiatric view which regards hoarding behaviour as a reflection of a deep "need" for love and security. Presumably, no "real" behavioural change was possible without meeting the patient's "needs" first. Even after the patient discontinued hoarding towels in her room, some nurses predicted that the change would not last and that worse behavior would replace it. Using a time sampling technique the patient was under continuous observation for over a year after the termination of the satiation programme. Not once during this period did the patient return to hoarding towels. Furthermore, no other behaviour problem replaced hoarding (1963).

In one part of an earlier study (Ayllon & Michael, 1959) the satiation technique was also used. The problem in this case involved three mentally defective patients who collected papers, magazines, and assorted rubbish which they carried about with them. Frequently they carried these items inside their clothes, which caused skin rashes that added to the general problem.

It was believed by some of the hospital personnel that the hoarding was reinforced by the attention which accrued to the patients because of their behavior, as well as by the real scarcity of printed material on the ward. Following the acknowledged effects of satiation in the laboratory, the experimenters felt that "flooding" the ward with magazines would have a similar effect on the behavior of the patients. Also, in order to expedite the elimination of hoarding, social reinforcement was withheld when hoarding was observed.

This satiation and extinction procedure was continued over a period of nine weeks, and the behavior of all the subjects was similar. There was a gradual trend of decreased hoarding, and by the end of nine weeks, hoarding was no longer a ward problem. Further, the problem did not recur over a six-month follow-up period.

As in other cases, some members of the nursing staff questioned the advisability of the satiation program. As one nurse argued, "behavior has its roots in the personality of the individual. The fact that he hoards so much indicates that Harry (one of the three hoarders) has a strong need for security. I don't see how we are going to change this need, and I also wonder if it is a good thing to do that." Apparently Harry did not "realize" that his behavior was rooted in his "personality," since (according to the report) upon completion of the program he would be found sitting in the dayroom looking at magazines rather than hoarding them.

In the final study to be reported in this series (Resnick, 1968), we turn again to one of our culture's more pervasive maladies, cigarette smoking. The satiation approach as used here is in sharp contrast to the methods usually proposed for the "cure," and it provides an interesting alternative solution to the problem.

Eight college students, all of whom had previously made unsuccessful attempts to stop smoking, volunteered to try this new program. Each had been smoking over a year (mean smoking time, 2.6 years), and each smoked at least one pack of cigarettes per day. Further, each subject expressed a sincere interest in stopping the "habit," and each one reported failure on earlier attempts.

The basic strategy outlined by Resnick was simple satiation, and the immediate goal of this outline was to bring each subject to a "satiation level" of four packs of cigarettes a day as quickly as possible. He intended that a subject should accomplish this within a week, and preferably within a few days.

On reporting to the experimenter after trying the program, one subject stated that he was unable to raise his smoking frequency above the usual level. A second subject maintained that she had tried satiation but had returned to her previous rate (a pack a day) two days later. The remaining six subjects showed fairly pronounced success with this technique and had not reinstated smoking after four months of abstinence.

These (very rapid) successes are most interesting, but, as the author points out, some extraneous factors could have produced the results by chance. Stimulus satiation, however, was the only variable which was systematically administered. In any event, the program had applied an established variable, and supplementary research would seem justified. After all, the effectiveness of satiation in helping a person with his cigarette problem is an empirical question.

In turning to the second half of this literature section, a few brief references to a series of cases reported by Goldiamond (1965) might illuminate the role of stimulus control in the modification and maintenance of behavior. One portion of his presentation of self-control procedures dealt with the "conjugal scene." This case involved a couple who did a great deal of bickering and arguing in their bedroom. Such behavior, of course, is often at odds with "lovemaking," and in this case it impeded the progress of these more tender emotions. The problem was to rearrange the bedroom stimuli so that new stimuli might set the occasion for amorous activity and decrease the probability of the occurrence of other incompatible activities. With this is view, the couple was instructed to purchase a yellow light and place it in the bedroom. Then, whenever each of the parties evidenced obvious sexual interest, they were to turn the yellow light on and give full vent to their desires. At all other times the yellow light was to remain off. In other words, the counselor's instructions had arranged for the three-term operant paradigm ($S^D - - \rightarrow R - - \rightarrow S^{R+}$). Sexual reinforcement was made contingent upon the occurrence of behavior only in the presence of the yellow light.

Stimulus control was also brought to bear in another marital case (Goldiamond, 1965). This case pertained to a sexual theme involving a "frustrated" wife. Apparently the couple (married ten years) indulged themselves sexually about twice a year. This very low frequency was unacceptable to the wife, and the marital relationship had begun to suffer as a consequence. The wife's attempts to entice her husband or to induce "extra" sexual interest met with failure. The therapist instituted a number of programs which also were singularly unsuccessful. Finally, another approach came to the therapist's attention. As Goldiamond wrote:

> Both Ss were extremely well-groomed. Their clothing was always in best array. The wife visited the beautician once a week and the

husband went to the barber every other week. In the session following the failure of control by the appointment book, the husband suggested that they might attach the opportunity to visit the beautician or barber as consequences to keeping the appointments (with each other). In the event that the appointments were not kept, the visits would not be allowed and could be resumed only when the appointments had been kept. His wife also felt that this would be extremely effective.

The next week they both showed up somewhat bedraggled. Thereafter, they were not bedraggled and the appointments were kept for the rest of that semester, at least (1965).

Here we see that the behavior to be established (the husband keeping appointments with his wife) had become a discriminative stimulus for other behaviors and reinforcements that were important to the couple. Keeping an appointment with one's mate had come to set the occasion for other reinforced responses (going to the beautician or barber, respectively).

Another case from the same article (Goldiamond, 1965) concerned a coed who had difficulty studying. Since the report is very brief and contains some interesting dialogue, it is reproduced below:

The program with the young lady started with human engineering of her desk. Since she felt sleepy when she studied, she was told to replace the 40-w lamp with a good one and to turn her desk away from her bed. It was also decided that her desk was to control study behavior. If she wished to write a letter, she should do so but in the dining room; if she wished to read comic books, she should do so but in the kitchen; if she wished to daydream, she should do so but was to go to another room; at her desk she was to engage in her school work and her school work only.

This girl had previously had a course in behavioral analysis and said, "I know what you're up to. You want that desk to assume stimulus control over me. I'm not going to let any piece of wood run my life for me."

"On the contrary," I said, "you want that desk to run you. It is you who decides when to put yourself under the control of your desk. It is like having a sharpened knife in a drawer. You decide when to use it: but when you want it, it is ready."

After the first week of the regimen, she came to me and gleefully said, "I spent only ten minutes at my desk last week."

"Did you study there?" I asked.

"Yes, I did," she said.

"Good," I said, "let's try to double that next week."

For the next few weeks we did not meet, but she subsequently reported that during the last month of the semester she was able to spend three hours a day at her desk for four weeks in a row, something she had been unable to do previously. When she sat at her desk she studied, and when she did other things she left her desk. The variable maintaining this increase in behavior as the semester drew to an end was apparently the forthcoming final examinations.

This completes our review of stimulus control. We will now turn to the remaining section and make some concluding comments on the techniques we presented over the last three chapters. We will also comment on the general applicability of conditioning procedures in the modification of operant behavior.

Summary and Evaluation of Operant Modification

One way of reviewing and summarizing the basic techniques used in the modification of operant behavior is simply to list the various operations that affect the probability of an organism's responding. Such a list provides a clear and succinct overview of the material covered in the preceding three chapters. To further emphasize this delineation, we have listed the stimulus manipulations under the relevant chapter headings:

Reinforcement and the Modification of Operant Behavior

One can strengthen a response by presenting a positive reinforcer immediately after the response is emitted.

One can eliminate a response by terminating the response-reinforcement contingency.

One can condition a completely new response through shaping—that is, by selectively reinforcing closer and closer approximations of the criterion response, and by extinguishing those of a lesser approximation.

Behavior maintained through reinforcement can be additionally modified by changing the schedule of reinforcement.

The Aversive Stimulus and Operant Behavior

One can strengthen a response by removing an aversive stimulus immediately after the response is emitted—that is, by negative reinforcement.

One can suppress a response through punishment. In the first instance of punishment, a response is suppressed when it is immediately followed by the presentation of an aversive stimulus.

In the second instance of punishment, a response is suppressed when it is immediately followed by the withdrawal of a positive reinforcer.

Other Variables in Operant Control

One can increase the probability of a response by first depriving the organism of a relevant stimulus.

One can decrease the probability of a response by first satiating the organism with a relevant simulus.

One can increase the probability of a response by presenting a discriminative stimulus.

One can decrease the probability of a response by removing the discriminative stimulus.

These are the basic operations in the control of operant behavior. Other techniques are simply variations of these operations or are more complex combinations of these approaches. *Chaining*, for example, is a term which indicates a sequence of behavior employing more than one specified discriminative stimulus, response, and reinforcer. It is, in fact, greatly in vogue in the acquisition and shaping of skills in "retardates." However, our purpose in this primer was to detail the basic variables and to foster a general knowledge of what is going on under the rubric of behavior modification. We could have also detailed related aspects of the behavior modification movement, but that would have been superfluous to our intent. As another instance, one might convincingly argue the position that drugs and other chemical agents play a major role in modification. And they do. This subject was not included because it would add nothing to what has already been discussed under basic operations. Some drugs satiate, and others affect the organism in the same way that deprivation does. Some drugs are used as positive reinforcers, while others function as aversive stimuli, and so on. In nearly all applications of chemical agents, their effect and function could be subsumed under one, or a combination, of the basic operations listed just a bit earlier.

The importance and the impact of the techniques discussed in the last three chapters cannot be overemphasized. Since most human behavior is operant, most human "problems" are also of an operant genesis and thereby subject to adjustment through principles of operant control. Moreover, as mentioned in Chapter 1, it is believed that most of the basic variables in the functional control of operant behavior are known. Further research, however, will provide new "insights" and new phenomena. Also, a careful quantification of the relevant parameters governing the relationship between environmental and behavioral variables will no doubt multiply the efficiency and effectiveness of the tools at hand. Nevertheless, the accomplishments and promise of contemporary behavior modification must be regarded by any objective observer as truly remarkable.

In reference to the limits of behavior modification techniques, a few comments should suffice. The "unintact" organism, the organism with a damaged or incomplete central nervous system, poses special problems. There are also certain biological factors that impose limits on operant methodologies. For example, one could muster this country's ten most sophisticated and learned behavior technologists, and provide them with unlimited funds, facilities, and time; yet, try as they might, it seems unlikely that they could ever condition an elephant to thread a needle. However, in view of the present accomplishments (and potential) of operant techniques in behavior modification, these minor types of limits will probably not markedly decrease anyone's general appreciation of the movement.

Selected Readings

There is no one book singularly appropriate to the topics in this chapter; however, we suggest that one's specific information in the subject matter of this chapter can be greatly expanded through the relevant sections of a variety of basic texts. Two of these, along with the pertinent sections, are listed below:

Lundin, R. W. *Personality: A behavioral analysis*. New York: Macmillan, 1969. See Chapters V and VII.

Skinner, B. F. *Science and human behavior*. (Paperback) New York: Free Press, 1965. See Chapters VII and IX.

The psychological journals most relevant to this chapter are:

Behaviour Research and Therapy

Journal of Applied Behavior Analysis

7

The Behavior Modification Movement

Contemporary Status

One way of assessing the virility of a scientific discipline or movement is by considering the amount of published material that bears directly on the content and orientation of that movement. But if a review covered all publications related to behavior modification, including works of a "basic research" sort on operant and respondent conditioning, the review would become quite burdensome. Even if the list of publications was limited only to areas in which behavior control is currently applied, it would still require a rather lengthy appendix to this primer. Rather than attempt any sort of comprehensive cataloging, we will confine ourselves only to the *most recent* books whose contents focus specifically on the modification of *maladaptive human behavior*. This review should be sufficient to provide the reader with a thorough appreciation of the dynamic growth which characterizes the movement, and it should also suggest to the reader means of expanding his knowledge in the area.

Perhaps the first book to have a major impact in promoting the behavior modification movement was *Psychotherapy by Reciprocal Inhibition* (Wolpe, 1958), which outlined a number of respondent modification techniques. This was followed by four books which covered research methodology as well as operant and respondent conditioning in the control of behavior. In order of appearance, these books are: *Conditioning*

Techniques in Clinical Practice and Research (Franks, 1964), *Research in Behavior Modification* (Krasner & Ullmann, 1965), *Case Studies in Behavior Modification* (Ullmann & Krasner, 1965), and *Control of Human Behavior* (Ulrich, Stachnik, & Mabry, 1966). Published at about the same time was a revised version of an earlier book on reciprocal inhibition, *Behavior Therapy Techniques* (Wolpe & Lazarus, 1966).

In the two succeeding years two other books made their appearance. The first was directed in its entirety to the modification of the behavior of children and was entitled *Child Development: Readings in Experimental Analysis* (Bijou & Baer, 1967). The second, *The Token Economy: A Motivational System for Therapy and Rehabilitation* (Ayllon & Azrin, 1968), dealt with the application of a broad conditioning program in an institutional setting.

Finally, in the early part of 1969, four other books pertinent to behavior modification were published. Wolpe, keeping abreast of continuing developments in reciprocal inhibition, authored *The Practice of Behavior Therapy*. In a similar vein, Franks offered a new systematic overview with his *Behavior Therapy: Appraisal and Status*. Along with these texts, two very comprehensive and encyclopedic books were completed. The first of these, Ullmann and Krasner's *A Psychological Approach to Abnormal Behavior*, offers a detailed reinterpretation of the entire field of "abnormal" psychology within the framework of experimental analysis and behavior modification. The second, Bandura's *Principles of Behavior Modification*, is more general in scope and application than earlier works of similar orientation.

Of course, the vitality of the behavior modification orientation finds expression in media other than books. Currently, most psychological periodicals concerned with research on "deviant" or "troublesome" human reactions and engagements are publishing studies on behavior modification. However, there are also two journals devoted exclusively to articles in this area. The first of these is *Behaviour Research and Therapy*, an international journal which has been published by the Pergamon Press since 1962. The second arrived on the scene in 1968. It is called the *Journal of Applied Behavior Analysis* and is published by the Society for the Experimental Analysis of Behavior.

Communication among those who are advocates of behavior modification is further encouraged through various meetings. These meetings are sponsored primarily by the national, regional, and state psychological associations; the Society for the Experimental Analysis of Behavior; and the Association for Advancement of Behavior Therapy. The activities of these groups increase yearly, and this growth is another indication of the vigor which characterizes behavior modification today.

Prospectus

It may be that the single most important aspect of the behavior modification movement is its emphasis on an operationally defined, readily observed, and easily measured dependent variable: behavior. In making behavior the focal object of "therapeutic" attention, rather than "conflict-resolution" or other "tinkerings" with the "mental" apparatus, behavior technologists have provided themselves with a most objective and sensitive indicant of their activities. The specificity of their criterion measure, behavioral change, lends itself to rather immediate evaluation of both the effects of their efforts and the rate at which they are progressing toward specific therapeutic goals. This one achievement takes "mental health" out of its historically hazy never-never land and places it fully within the pale of a natural science, directly subjecting it to the principles of conditioning.

Consequently, while much of the application of conditioning principles in behavior modification still entails a great deal of "art," the behavior therapy movement is supported by the substratum of a "hard core" scientific discipline. The art will be guided, modified, and improved with advances in basic and applied research in this domain. In contrast to many traditional and current therapies, the statements constituting behavior modification's "body of knowledge" are always empirical statements subject to empirical test. As such, the stated relationships between behavior, on the one hand, and the environmental variables of which behavior is a function, on the other, are also subject to the major criteria of any natural science: intersubjective testability and reliability. Within this frame, though incorrect statements about governing relationships *may* be made, such statements cannot endure. Over time, the probability that correct statements will prevail is assured.

While this evaluation may convince the novice to psychology of the general soundness of the behavior modification movement, its critics will not be so easily instructed. They will insist, for instance, that changing a patient's behavior has told us nothing about whether his "deeper" problem has been solved. In response to this, we would submit that when one's behavior has been "improved," there are no deeper problems. After all, how does the typical psychiatrist know that a patient is "well"? In the final analysis, though he may not recognize it, the psychiatrist's judgment of the patient's health is based not on "conflict-resolution" or on a strengthened "ego," but rather on what the patient says and does—on his behavior.

Then too, as seen in some of the pages of this book, many mental health personnel view the direct control of human behavior—even the modification of maladaptive behavior—as ominous, threatening, and somehow "unnatural." Further, to deprive a person of food or to soil his clothes deliberately is often viewed as an example of patient-abuse. It is somewhat ironic that the continued administration of drugs, electro-shock therapy, or a prefrontal lobotomy is not viewed in the same vein. Surely, if a patient is suffering from a carcinogenic tumor, surgery is the most efficient and, in the long run, "kindest" course of action. Few people would argue that giving such a patient love and warmth—while offering "chants" and "flower petals" for his recovery—should supersede surgery. Yet, in behavior modification the parallel of this argument often prevails. Our position on this issue is simply this: That action which most quickly, efficiently, and enduringly dissolves the patient's discomforts, makes his behavior more adaptive, and permits him to function more adequately is the most humanistic course.

There are, of course, many other issues and attitudes which divide the traditional therapist and the behavior technologist. At the empirical level, for instance, there is the pseudo-problem of "symptom substitution," which has not ceased to rankle quite a few members of the "traditionalist" camp. In another area of controversy, the issue of ethics in the control of human behavior finds few people assuming a "middle-of-the-road" position. But however much import these issues may carry, we feel that they are not within the scope of a primer. In regard to these and other questions, the reader is directed to supplementary source materials.

As is often the case, the questions and issues which divide today's "mental health" professionals will not likely be resolved by attempts to clarify the various positions. Perhaps, after all, such a resolution through verbal interaction is really unimportant. The most basic issues can be reduced to empirical questions, and the acceptance of behavior modification will in large part depend upon the results of future research. In any event, the most powerful argument for its endorsement by any given therapist rests with the most basic variable of operant control: reinforcement. The behavior of the therapist who successfully employs behavior modification techniques will be shaped in directions that support the movement. In all of this world there is no controlling agent as forceful, yet quite as gentle, as positive reinforcement.

Selected Readings

For the reader who would like to pursue the subject of this primer in great depth and breadth, the following two texts are recommended. Both go considerably beyond the borders of the primer and detail the entire behavior therapy-modification spectrum including history, philosophy, and issues. They also offer a wider and more complex application of the basic techniques we have discussed.

Bandura, A. *Principles of behavior modification*. New York: Holt, 1969.

Ullmann, L. P., & Krasner, L. *A psychological approach to abnormal behavior*. Englewood Cliffs, N. J.: Prentice-Hall, 1969.

Hospital & Community Psychiatry, a journal of the American Psychiatric Association, published a sequence of articles in 1968 on the "ethics" issue. They provide interesting reading about some of the problems or pseudo-problems discussed in the behavior therapy literature today. Rather than alphabetize the list by author, we will present the series of articles as they were published in *Hospital & Community Psychiatry*. The first article appeared in the journal's February 1968 issue; the others appeared in the July 1968 issue under the heading "Issues and Implications of Operant Conditioning."

Lucero, R. J., Vail, D. J., & Scherber, J. Regulating operant-conditioning programs. Pp. 53-54.

Miron, N. B. The primary ethical consideration. Pp. 226-227.

Cahoon, D. D. Balancing procedures against outcomes. Pp. 228-229.

Bragg, R. A., & Wagner, M. K. Can deprivation be justified? Pp. 229-230.

Ball, T. S. The re-establishment of social behavior. Pp. 230-232.

Lucero, R. J., & Vail, D. J. Public policy and public responsibility. Pp. 232-233.

The following articles are provided for those readers who would like to become more keenly aware of some of the broader issues and concerns associated with the behavior modification movement.

Cahoon, D. D. Symptom substitution and the behavior therapies: A reappraisal. *Psychological Bulletin*, 1968, **69** 149-156.

Krasner, L. Behavior control and social responsibility. *American Psychologist*, 1964, **17**, 199-204.

Rogers, C. R., & Skinner, B. F. Some issues concerning the control of human behavior: A symposium. *Science*, 1956, **124**, 1057-1066.

Skinner, B. F. Freedom and the control of men. *American Scholar*, 1955-56, Winter, **25**, Special Issue, 47-65.

Glossary

Those terms and concepts that are germane to the scientific substratum and epistemological base of behavior modification are defined and explained within the framework of radical behaviorism. This treatment is given to most of the terminology associated with the variables and principles pertinent to respondent and operant conditioning. Precise, consistent, and systematic definitions are required for this portion of the primer's subject domain, since it is the core of behavior technology. Other terms, primarily those referring to diagnostic classification and more general psychological jargon, are given broader, traditional definitions. While these terms also could be revised to fit into the pale of radical behaviorism, it would not advance the major purpose of the primer. Moreover, such a reinterpretation of all the terms of the primer during the student's initiation to behavior modification might well impede rather than promote his progress. In order to maintain a clear distinction between the two "kinds" of definitions used in the Glossary, the author has marked the broader, "traditional" definitions with an asterisk.

Adaptive Behavior—Behavior which is regarded as appropriate in a given context; behavior which results in an individual's effective interpersonal and environmental interaction. Adaptive responses are those which do not result in abrasion or discomfort to the behaving organism, and which do not precipitate intervention into the individual's life by some authority or other responsible social agent.

*Affective Reaction—A reaction characterized by exaggeration and inappropriateness of mood and emotion; often accompanied by thought disturbance.

*Analytic Therapy—In its more specific usage, the systematic psychology developed by Carl Jung. As used in the primer, analytic therapy is a broad, generic term referring to the wide variety of Freudian and neo-Freudian therapeutic procedures and orientations. These procedures may include one or more of the therapeutic techniques of free-association, dream interpretation, and analysis of the patient's speech content.

*Anxiety—A general feeling of uneasiness, dread, and apprehension about what might happen. While fear usually involves some object, person, or situation which the individual can identify as the cause of his discomfort, anxiety is less specific and typically more irrational. The feelings which characterize anxiety are also concomitant with changes in responses mediated by the autonomic nervous system.

*Autosuggestion—This term refers to behavior that an organism controls through self-suggestion. The term often implies that some quasi-hypnotic procedure was involved in establishing the suggestion.

Aversive Stimulus—Any stimulus which the organism will terminate or avoid if given the opportunity. Consequently, an aversive stimulus is one which is central to the operation of *negative reinforcement.*

Avoidance Behavior—The behavior of an organism which either postpones or avoids the occurrence of an aversive stimulus.

Basic Variable—Any single variable which can be isolated and shown to be operative in the formulation of first-order empirical laws; those variables which enter into the functional relationships of any subject matter or system at the empirical, observational level.

Behavior—Any elicited or emitted activity of an organism that is observable, or potentially observable, by another organism. This definition includes those responses that are mediated by the autonomic nervous system (involving the smooth muscles and glands), as well as responses controlled by the central nervous system and represented both by movements of the skeletal muscles and by the associated interaction of the organism with its environment.

Behavioral Model—*See* **Psychological Model**

Behavioral Repertoire—The sum total of all the responses, operant or respondent, which may be evidenced in any given organism. As a general rule, however, the term refers to the totality of the individual's operant repertoire.

*Catatonic Schizophrenia—A type of schizophrenic reaction in which the individual displays conspicuous and excessive motor activity or generalized inhibition and stupor.

Chaining—A procedure in which one operant response leads to another. The procedure involves a "linking" of the typical three-term operant paradigm (discriminative stimulus, response, reinforcement), which permits the development of a series of connected operants of indefinite length.

*Chronic Schizophrenia—A schizophrenic reaction of long duration.

*Compulsion—A strong, sometimes uncontrollable, "urge" to engage in some particular act. The act is often contrary to the individual's sense of "right and wrong."

Conditioned Emotional Reaction—An emotion or emotional reaction brought about through learning.

Conditioned Response—(Respondent) A response elicited by a conditioned stimulus—that is, by a formerly neutral stimulus which has been repeatedly paired with an unconditioned stimulus. (Operant) A response which has increased in "strength" (frequency) because it has been succeeded by reinforcement.

Conditioned Stimulus—A stimulus which has acquired the power to elicit a response (the respondent case), or one which has acquired the power to reinforce a response (the operant case).

Conditioning—(Respondent) The process of pairing a neutral stimulus with an unconditioned stimulus. The result of this process is that, after a number of pairings, the neutral stimulus will itself come to elicit the response formerly elicited by the unconditioned stimulus. (Operant) The process in which a reinforcing stimulus immediately follows an emitted response. The result of this response-reinforcement contingency is that the response will gain in "strength"; that is, its frequency or probability of occurrence will increase.

*Conflict—A mental crisis precipitated by the simultaneous occurrence of two or more antagonistic "motives" or "impulses."

Counterconditioning—The establishment of a stimulus-response "connection" in which the new response is incompatible with the response formerly elicited by the stimulus. This term is generally limited to the case of respondent conditioning, though a similar process can be arranged for operants.

Criterion Measure—A standard by which one may assess the relative effects of one or more independent variables on the dependent variable under investigation. For instance, if a subject or patient had a fear of rats, and the independent variable was ten sessions of systematic desensitization, the criterion measure for the success of therapy might be whether or not the subject could touch a rat in a post-therapy test.

*Delusion—A false and erroneous belief, or system of beliefs, which cannot be modified or changed either through reasoning with the individual holding them or by displaying facts contradicting them.

*Depressive Reaction—A neurotic reaction characterized by extreme and unusual depression. Associated with the depression, one frequently finds anxiety, self-depreciation, and other negative ruminations.

Differential Reinforcement—A term indicating that among a host of responses emitted, certain specified responses are reinforced while the others are not reinforced.

Discriminative Stimulus—A stimulus which sets the occasion for reinforced responding. Stimulus control of this sort is brought about when responses are reinforced in the presence of a specified stimulus and not otherwise. As a result of this procedure, the stimulus gains control over the probability that the response will be emitted.

Drive—A summary term for two basic manipulations. The first of these, the deprivation-satiation dimension, involves depriving an organism of a reinforcing stimulus. The second manipulation involves the presentation of an aversive stimulus. In both instances, the most important effect of drive is to make the reinforcement operation possible.

*Ego—A Freudian term meaning, in the broader sense, the self or the individual's self-concept. In the stricter Freudian meaning of the term, the ego is the mediator between the id and the superego. Other functions of the ego are to engage in reality testing and to distinguish between the self and the environment.

*Electro-Shock Therapy—A form of therapy in which weak electric currents are applied to the head, producing convulsions and unconsciousness. It is assumed to alleviate some psychopathological symptomatology.

*EMG (Electromyogram)—A recording of the action currents in a muscle.

*Emotional Reaction—This term refers to the expression of emotions and to the autonomic responses which accompany them. The "emotional" individual is one who is easily stimulated and who expresses frequent, and often intense, emotional change.

Escape Behavior—A response, or chain of responses, which is reinforced or maintained by the termination of an aversive stimulus.

Extinction—A process whereby a conditioned response is reduced to its preconditioned level or strength, often approaching or reaching zero magnitude or frequency. The process of extinction in the case of respondents involves continuing presentation of the conditioned stimulus without any further pairing with the unconditioned stimulus. With operant responses, extinction results when responding is no longer followed by reinforcement.

*Free Association—A therapeutic technique, developed by Sigmund Freud, in which the patient is instructed to say anything that comes into his mind, irrespective of how trivial, embarrassing, or inconsequential it might appear at the moment.

Free Operant—An operant response that is not under the control of a discriminative stimulus.

Functional Relation—In current scientific psychology this term has replaced the traditional "cause and effect" relation. It simply means that there is an established relationship between a dependent and an independent variable, so that when the independent variable occurs there will be a change in the dependent variable. Causality, because of certain philosophical meanings associated with the term, is not implied.

*Id—A Freudian term signifying that part of the mind which seats the libido. The id is not in contact with reality and is governed entirely by the search for pleasure, regardless of the consequences. The id is often in conflict with the ego.

Incompatible Response—Responses which cannot occur simultaneously, though each may be elicited by the same stimulus situation; e.g., laughing is incompatible with crying, joy is incompatible with sorrow, and relaxation is incompatible with anxiety.

Intermittent Reinforcement—Any reinforcement schedule in which responses are not reinforced after each occurrence of the response.

Intersubjective Testability—Characteristic of an event or a relationship that can be ascertained by any qualified observer. This term, in the parlance of philosophers of science, has superseded an earlier term of similar meaning: objectivity. It refers primarily to phenomena holding empirical status and is one of the criteria of statements that fall within the realm of any natural science.

Maladaptive Behavior—Behavior which is ineffective or inappropriate in a given context, and which results in an individual's ineffectiveness in his interpersonal and environmental interactions. More specific to this primer, maladaptive responses are those which lead to an individual's felt discomfort and distress or to intervention into the person's life by some authority or other responsible social agency.

*Medical Model—The medical model of "mental illness" holds that "abnormal" behavior is the result of, or is caused by, some internal entity. This internal entity is usually regarded as physical in nature and is made analogous to other diseases in which the malady is underlied by germs, viruses, lesions, and other pathogenic agents. In this model, the "abnormal" behavior is regarded as merely a symptom precipitated by the internal "disease" entity. The medical model of "mental illness" also precludes the direct "treatment" or modification of behavior itself. Rather, the medical (psychiatric) view dictates that behavior change cannot be made unless the presumed internal, underlying pathology is first alleviated.

Negative Reinforcement—The increase in the frequency of emission of a response, or the maintenance of a response, when the consequence of the response is termination or avoidance of an aversive stimulus. A response is negatively reinforced if it results in termination or avoidance of an aversive stimulus.

*Neurosis—A disorder characterized by poor insight regarding the nature of one's problems and by conflicts, anxiety, personality impairment, and other psychopathological symptomatology.

*Neurotic—An individual who is suffering from a neurosis. The term also refers to behavior which is symptomatic of a neurosis.

Neutral Stimulus—A stimulus which is not immediately affecting the organism in some specified manner. A stimulus, which, at a given moment, is not in control of some specified response of the organism.

***Obsession**—An irrational and persistent idea or preoccupation.

***Obsessive-Compulsive Neurosis**—A neurosis characterized by persistent and often discomforting "ideas," accompanied by "urges" and "impulses" to put the ideas into action. These ideas are generally quite irrational, and the acts associated with them are inappropriate and maladaptive.

Operant Behavior—Behavior mediated by the central nervous system and involving, primarily, the skeletal musculature. Operant responses act on, and interact with, the environment and are controlled and modified by the principles of operant conditioning. Operant responding includes not only the gross motor movements of the organism but also its verbal behavior. Most of the daily, ongoing behavior of the individual as he interacts with his environment and other people is operant in nature.

Operational Definition—A definition in which the central term is given meaning by reference to some very specific operation or procedure. For example, an operational definition of hunger might be: We deprived our subjects of food for twelve hours. An operational definition of intelligence, as a second example, might be: Intelligence was measured by the full-scale I.Q. score obtained on the Wechsler Adult Intelligence Scale. In either case, the only meaning attending the term is in the operation or procedure involved in distinguishing it from other terms.

***Opposite Speech**—The tendency for some people (for instance, patients diagnosed as schizophrenic) to say the opposite of what they "mean" and to respond contrary to their wishes and wants.

***Pan-Anxiety**—A very broad, unusually generalized, free-floating anxiety.

Parameters—All of the variables, beyond those being considered at the moment, which do have some influence on the dependent variable under scrutiny.

***Paranoiac**—One who suffers from paranoia or paranoid schizophrenia.

***Paranoid Schizophrenia**—A few of the major characteristics of this form of "mental illness" are delusions of grandeur or persecution, intellectual deterioration, and disturbances of thinking (including hallucinations).

***Pathological Condition**—A condition of disease, disorder, or disturbance which interferes with "normal" and adaptive functioning.

***Personality Disorder**—A diagnostic category which includes persons showing difficulty in their social adjustment. These difficulties are reflected through inadequacies in motivational and emotional processes, and may result in schizoid, paranoid, and sociopathic disturbances.

***Phobia**—A fear elicited by a specific stimulus or situation which is strong, persistent, and irrational.

Positive Reinforcement—The operation in which the presentation of a stimulus as the consequence of a response will increase the strength (frequency) of that response.

*Prefrontal Lobotomy—A surgical operation on a part of the brain; designed to alleviate certain psychotic symptoms.

Premack Principle—This principle states that if behavior X is of higher probability than behavior Y, then behavior Y can be made more probable by making behavior X contingent upon it.

Primary Reinforcer—An "unlearned" reinforcing stimulus. A stimulus that will function as a reinforcer without prior learning on the part of the organism. Its reinforcing efficacy derives from the biological characteristics of the organism. For example, food, water, sex, and the termination of aversive stimuli are primary reinforcers.

*Pseudonecrophilia—Erotic fantasies related to dead bodies; sometimes accompanied by masturbation.

*Psychiatry—A branch of medicine that focuses on the diagnosis, treatment, and prevention of "mental illness."

*Psychoanalysis—A systematic approach to the understanding and cure of "mental" disorders; developed (originally) by Sigmund Freud. This view holds that the "roots" of human behavior are to be found in unconscious motivation and conflict.

*Psychodynamic—Refers to psychoanalytic and other "depth" psychologies. The term also implies a major concern with the study of emotional and motivational processes.

Psychological Model—Assumes that most behavior, including that which is classified as abnormal, is learned. An additional assumption is that the major variables of which behavior is a function are to be found in the organism's environment, and that a manipulation of these variables will produce the appropriate modifications in the organism's behavior.

*Psychosis—A relatively severe disorder, the symptoms of which include: disorganization of thought; emotional disturbance; disorientation regarding time, space, and person; hallucinations; and delusions.

Punishment—This term refers to two basic operations. The first form of punishment occurs when an aversive stimulus is presented as the consequence of a response. The second form of punishment occurs when a positive reinforcer is withheld or withdrawn as the consequence of a response.

Radical Behaviorism—The position of the radical behaviorist is that the locus of all major variables of which behavior is a function is the organism's environment. In addition, the radical behaviorist would state that the functional relations which obtain between environmental and behavioral variables will provide for all the laws required for an account of an organism's behavior. This position does not imply, for example, that certain biological and physical characteristics do not limit the effectiveness of these environmental variables in some cases. For instance, it does seem improbable that the average 90-pound "weakling" will ever make the first-string varsity football squad at the University of Michigan, no matter how much food, water, sex, or money is made contingent upon such an accomplishment.

Reinforcement—One of the operations which will increase the strength of a response. In operant conditioning, reinforcement refers to an operation which follows the emission of a response. The term is also applied to respondents, though the usage is less frequent. In the respondent case, reinforcement refers to pairing an unconditioned stimulus with a conditioned or a neutral stimulus.

Reinforcer—Any stimulus which can be used to increase the strength of the response which precedes it.

Reliability—One of the major criteria of any statement that is to be admitted into the content of a natural science. It means that the observation to which the statement applies must be recurrent and subject to reproduction whenever the conditions which originally produced it prevail.

Respondent Behavior—Stimulus-elicited behavior that is usually mediated by the autonomic nervous system, involving reactions of the smooth muscles and glands.

Response—As employed in this book, response is synonymous with behavior and refers to observable and measurable movements of the organism. These movements include glandular and smooth muscle reactions and effects, as well as external, motor movements and their effects.

Response Strength—As used here, response strength is a summary term for the frequency of occurrence of an operant and for the latency or magnitude of a respondent.

Schedules of Reinforcement—A term used as a general rubric for (1) the varieties of ways in which reinforcers can be presented to the organism and (2) the infinite number of response-reinforcement contingencies. A few of the most elementary schedules are: *Continuous* (each response is reinforced); *Fixed Ratio* (a response is reinforced after some specified and constant number of responses have been emitted); *Variable Ratio* (a response is reinforced after some specified but varying number of responses have been emitted); *Fixed Interval* (a response is reinforced after the passage of some specified and constant period of time); and *Variable Interval* (a response is reinforced after some specified but varying period of time).

*Schizoid Personality—A person with a schizoid personality is excessively withdrawn from other people and his general environment. He also has considerable difficulty in expressing himself or engaging in any social interaction.

*Schizophrenia—A group of psychotic reactions. Some of the major symptoms are withdrawal, emotional and affective disturbances, hallucinations, delusions, and progressive mental deterioration.

Selective Reinforcement—*See* **Differential Reinforcement.**

Shaping—The process in which reinforcement is differentially applied to those responses that constitute a closer and closer approximation to the ultimate response one wishes to bring about.

Stimulus—A generic term for any environmental or internal event or condition, including the organism's own behavior. Some specific terms included in this category are reinforcing stimulus, conditioned stimulus, unconditioned stimulus, eliciting stimulus, discriminative stimulus, and neutral stimulus.

Stimulus Control—*See* **Discriminative Stimulus.**

Stimulus Generalization—The phenomenon of a gradient of responding to neutral—i.e., unpaired or non-reinforced—stimuli that "resemble" the conditioned stimulus or the discriminative stimulus. Those stimuli which most closely "resemble" the original conditioned stimulus or discriminative stimulus produce a greater generalized response than those which are less similar.

Strength of a Response—*See* **Response Strength.**

Successive Approximation—*See* **Shaping.**

*****Superego**—A Freudian term representing that part of the personality which is equivalent, in the popular vernacular, to conscience. It is the third term in the Freudian personality triad of id, ego, and superego.

*****Symptom Substitution**—The belief held by many traditional therapists, particularly those of a psychoanalytic persuasion, that if one "treats" the symptom of a "mental" disturbance, then the underlying "cause" of the disturbance will precipitate some new symptom in place of the one ameliorated.

*****Traditional Therapy**—As used in this primer, a broad reference to most non-behavior modification techniques. However, the more specific allusion is to those therapies that regard "abnormal" behavior as symptomatic of some internal pathology which reflects itself in some form of behavioral disruption.

Variable—Any behavior or behavior property, and any stimulus condition, which may be quantified or which varies in at least two ways; e.g., hours of food deprivation, sex (male or female), number of reinforced responses, rate of bar-pressing.

References

Ayllon, T. Intensive treatment of psychotic behavior by stimulus satiation and food reinforcement. *Behaviour Research and Therapy*, 1963, 1, 53-61.

Ayllon, T., & Azrin, N. H. *The token economy: A motivational system for therapy and rehabilitation*. New York: Appleton-Century-Crofts, 1968.

Ayllon, T., & Michael, J. The psychiatric nurse as a behavioral engineer. *Journal of the Experimental Analysis of Behavior*, 1959, 2, 323-334.

Bandura, A. *Principles of behavior modification*. New York: Holt, 1969.

Bijou, S. W., & Baer, D. M. (Eds.) *Child development: Readings in experimental analysis*. New York: Appleton-Century-Crofts, 1967.

Cowden, R. C., & Ford, L. I. Systematic desensitization with phobic schizophrenics. *The American Journal of Psychiatry*, 1962, 119, 241-245.

Franks, C. M. *Behavior therapy: Appraisal and status*. New York: McGraw-Hill, 1969.

Franks, C. M. *Conditioning techniques in clinical practice and research*. New York: Springer, 1964.

Fuller, P. R. Operant conditioning of a vegetative human organism. *American Journal of Psychology*, 1949, 29, 587-590.

Geer, J. H., & Silverman, I. Treatment of a recurrent nightmare by behavior modification procedures. *Journal of Abnormal Psychology*, 1967, 72, 188-190.

Goldiamond, I. Self control procedures and personal behavior problems. *Psychological Reports* 1965, **17**, 851-868.

Haughton, E., & Ayllon, T. Production and elimination of symptomatic behavior. In L. P. Ullmann and L. Krasner (Eds.), *Case studies in behavior modification*. New York: Holt, 1965.

Hogan, R. A. Implosive therapy in the short term treatment of psychotics. *Psychotherapy: Theory, Research, and Practice*, 1966, **3**, 25-32.

Hogan, R. A., & Kirchner, J. H. Preliminary report of the extinction of learned fears via short term implosive therapy. *Journal of Abnormal Psychology*, 1967, **72**, 106-109.

Homme, L. E., deBaca, P. C., Deirue, J. V., Steinhorst, R., & Rickert, E. J. Use of the Premack principle in controlling the behavior of nursery school children. *Journal of the Experimental Analysis of Behavior*, 1963, 6, 544.

Isaacs, W., Thomas, J., & Goldiamond, I. Application of operant conditioning to reinstate verbal behavior in psychotics. *Journal of Speech and Hearing Disorders*, 1960, **25**, 8-12.

Jacobson, E. *Progressive relaxation*. Chicago: University of Chicago Press, 1938.

Jones, M. C. Elimination of children's fears. *Journal of Experimental Psychology*, 1924, **7**, 382-390.

Krasner, L., & Ullmann, L. P. (Eds.) *Research in behavior modification*. New York: Holt, 1965.

Kushner, M. Desensitization of a post-traumatic phobia. In L. P. Ullmann and L. Krasner (Eds.), *Case studies in behavior modification*. New York: Holt, 1965.

Lazarus, A. A. A case of pseudonecrophilia treated by behavior therapy. *Journal of Clinical Psychology*, 1968, **24**, 113-115.

Levis, D. J., & Carrera, R. Effects of ten hours of implosive therapy in the treatment of outpatients: A preliminary report. *Journal of Abnormal Psychology*, 1967, **72**, 504-508.

Premack, D. Toward empirical laws: I. Positive reinforcement. *Psychological Review*, 1959, **66**, 219-233.

Resnick, J. H. The control of smoking behavior by stimulus satiation. *Behaviour Research and Therapy*, 1968, **6**, 113-114.

Skinner, B. F. *Science and human behavior*. New York: Macmillan, 1953.

Stampfl, T. G., & Levis, D. J. Essentials of implosive therapy: A learning-theory-based psychodynamic behavior therapy. *Journal of Abnormal Psychology*, 1967, **72**, 496-503.

Sulzer, E. S. Behavior modification in adult psychiatric patients. In L. P. Ullmann and L. Krasner (Eds.), *Case studies in behavior modification*. New York: Holt, 1965.

References

Ullmann, L. P., & Krasner, L. *A psychological approach to abnormal behavior*. Englewood Cliffs, N. J.: Prentice-Hall, 1969.

Ullmann, L. P., & Krasner, L. (Eds.) *Case studies in behavior modification*. New York: Holt, 1965.

Ulrich, R., Stachnik, T., & Mabry, J. (Eds.) *Control of human behavior*. Glenview, Ill.: Scott, Foresman, 1966.

Wilde, G. J. S. Behaviour therapy for addicted cigarette smokers: A preliminary investigation. *Behaviour Research and Therapy*, 1964, **2**, 107-109.

Williams, C. D. The elimination of tantrum behavior by extinction procedures. *Journal of Abnormal and Social Psychology*, 1959, **59**, 269.

Wilson, A., & Smith, F. J. Counterconditioning therapy using free association: A pilot study. *Journal of Abnormal Psychology*, 1968, **73**, 474-478.

Wolpe, J. *Psychotherapy by reciprocal inhibition*. Stanford, Calif.: Stanford University Press, 1958.

Wolpe, J. *The practice of behavior therapy*. Elmsford, N. Y.: Pergamon, 1969.

Wolpe, J. & Lazarus, A. A. *Behavior therapy techniques*. Elmsford, N.Y.: Pergamon, 1966.

Index